SEASON'S BOUNTY

For my mother, Engela,
and my grandmothers,
Josephine and Sophia ...
The seeds you planted
have sprouted!

SEASON'S BOUNTY

Cooking with nature's abundance

SOPHIA LINDOP

BOOK**STORM**

CONTENTS

FOREWORD

To have had our knees under Sophia and Paddy Lindop's table as often as we have has been a rare pleasure for Maddy and me. At their Cape Town home, tucked away in the shadow of Table Mountain, the food is delicious and sophisticated like the perfect lamb cutlet baked on a slice of baguette à la Provençale. On their farm, midst the peace of the great plains of the Karoo, the food is rustic and wholesome, pigs' cheek with apple and cider, and a tranche of cheese from Gay's Guernsey Dairy in Prince Albert. And always accompanied by the 'perfect match' wines from Paddy's cellar.

Sophia and I have worked together for some five years, and I am thrilled to see the fruits of her prodigious talents on the pages of this book. Her food is intuitive and instinctive and comes from her rich Afrikaans and Lebanese past. What better combination could there be?

Michael Olivier
Cape Town, 2014

———— • ————

One of the drawbacks of being a professional chef is that no one ever wants to invite you for dinner – I suppose most people find it intimidating. But not Sophia. She is a crazy pack of dynamite. She exudes confidence and once in her kitchen she turns from sultry Mediterranean vixen into a lightning-wielding Zeus – and when you are invited to her house for dinner, you had better come hungry.

Sophia has always been a passionate, enthusiastic and generous person, and these traits are reflected in her cooking. It is always a treat to sit at her table and, no matter what she's in the mood to conjure up, there's always something authentic and heartfelt about her food. You really can taste the love.

This book is the next best thing to being invited over to Sophia's, and I can only hope that you get as much pleasure out of the recipes as I have had around the table with Sophia and Paddy. The food is as bountiful as it is beautiful, and as honest as the day is long – enjoy!

Pete Goffe-Wood
Cape Town, 2014

A TASTE FOR ALL SEASONS

I came into this world on an irrigation farm in a little village called Douglas, in the Northern Cape province of South Africa. My father is of Lebanese descent, and my mother, born into a conservative Afrikaans family, hailed from Cape Town.

I was born into a cloud of cooking aromas and my earliest memories are of women and laughter in the kitchens of their respective homes. All the women in my family were skilled and enthusiastic cooks, but the three most prominent influences came from my Lebanese grandmother, my Afrikaans ouma, and my mother.

Being the only daughter in a Lebanese household came with certain expectations – happily, at the age of five I began to show a keen interest in cooking, an interest fostered by all around me. Never slow to rise to the occasion, my grandfather produced two sturdy wooden boxes – one for my grandmother (not much taller than I was at that time) and one for me – so that we could reach the stove and together begin my journey into the world of food. My Lebanese grandmother lived to cook. She was always ready in case someone popped by, and in the tradition of true Lebanese hospitality, would forcefully encourage them to sit down, unwind and enjoy a meal. My grandfather was the village doctor, and some of his patients would conveniently schedule an appointment with him so that it could be followed by a visit and a meal with my grandmother – a holistic approach to true healing that can only take place over a plate of good food! It was in the kitchen of my Lebanese grandmother that I was taught to use my intuition – something that influences my cooking to this day – and where the smell of garlic became synonymous with the smell of home.

My Afrikaans ouma was a woman of the earth, and her food was wholesome and seasonal. She instilled in me a passion for growing my own vegetables and herbs, and for using what is in season. To this day I describe my style as 'earthy'. Her pot-roasted lamb and potatoes were legendary, and the flavours are still vivid in my memory.

But it was my mother who was the real whizz, the one who understood the Psychology of Cooking! She also understood her rebellious and fiercely independent middle child and only daughter. And it was in her kitchen that I learnt to believe in my ability to cook. At the age of five I began to stir and taste, and to watch and absorb a passion that ran very deep. I will never forget my first solo meal at age seven, after a two-year apprenticeship in the many family kitchens. That evening my mother, in all her wisdom, made an encouraging comment about my dish that gave me the wings to fly – and I have never looked back!

I later studied food and wine for six years, but I always feel that the formal training only provided the words for a song that had been playing in my heart for a very long time. My life has been filled with adventure and detours, but in the end I was led back to my kitchen, where I feel so at home!

As I sit here today, the smell of a Northern Cape lamb shoulder pot-roasting with carrots, garlic (of course), sundried tomatoes, red onion and homemade preserved lemons draped around me like a warm, familiar blanket on this cold day, I think with nostalgia of these three amazing women and how they shaped my life.

And so, here it is. It is done. Please accept this invitation into my kitchen, my life, my childhood and my heart – I trust that this book will inspire you to love food, to get to know where the ingredients come from, and to bless one another by sharing meals.

Sophia
Cape Town, 2014

NOTE

— • —

For easy cooking that does not demand too much thought about the metric conversions,
I have used the following basic measures.

1 cup = 250 ml | 1 tbsp = 15 ml | 1 tsp = 5 ml

— • —

The following also indicate whether a dish is vegetarian, gluten free or low carb.

 (V) – vegetarian | (GF) – gluten free | (LC) – low carb or even carb free

SPRING

— • —

NAARTJIES 10 | ASPARAGUS 16

CARROTS 22 | BANANAS 28

AVOCADOS 32 | LEMONS 38

— • —

Spring is probably my favourite season. I love
the fragrant blossoms that burst open in the
orchards, filling the air with the promise of fruit.
One of my most cherished memories is of my
ouma's puffed-up milk tart, delicately infused
with naartjie peel.

Baked naartjie and crottin (recipe on page 10)

BAKED NAARTJIE AND CROTTIN

(V) | (GF) | (LC) | SERVES *6* | DIFFICULTY *quick and easy* | PREPARATION TIME *20 minutes*

100 g crottin
3 naartjies
6 drops orange-blossom water
  (2 drops per naartjie)

Preheat the oven to 180 °C.

Cut the crottin into 6 even slices. Cut the naartjies in half, add the drops of orange-blossom water and place a slice of the crottin on each naartjie half.

Place the naartjies on baking paper on an oven tray in the preheated oven. Bake for 15 minutes, and serve as part of a cheese board.

See image on page 9.

NAARTJIE CHICKEN WINGS

(GF) | (LC) | SERVES *4 as a snack* | DIFFICULTY *quick and easy* | PREPARATION TIME *50 minutes*

10 chicken wings
olive oil
generous sprinkling Portuguese
  chicken spice
juice of 3 large naartjies
2 naartjies, halved

Preheat the oven to 200 °C.

Rub the chicken wings with the olive oil. Sprinkle the spice over and place in an oven dish. Drizzle the naartjie juice over the chicken wings and tuck the halved naartjies in between the chicken pieces.

Roast for 40 minutes and a further 5 minutes under the grill until they are golden and crispy. Serve as a snack with drinks.

Naartjie chicken wings

NAARTJIE CRÈME BRÛLÉE

(v) | (GF) | SERVES *8* | DIFFICULTY *moderate* | PREPARATION TIME *50 minutes*

1 whole egg
5 egg yolks
100 g caster sugar
125 ml milk
375 ml cream
4 tbsp naartjie juice
peel of 1 naartjie
6 tbsp white sugar for
    caramelising

Preheat the oven to 130 °C.

Beat the whole egg, egg yolks and caster sugar together until the mixture turns a pale yellow colour.

Slowly bring the milk and cream, along with the naartjie juice and the peel, to a gentle boil. As soon as it begins to boil, remove from the heat, remove the peel and slowly add the hot mixture to the egg mixture, using a metal spoon, stirring all the time. Pour this back into the pot, and place the peel back in the mixture. Cook on the stove at a medium to low heat. Stir the mixture with a metal spoon until it coats the back of the spoon – usually after about 10 to 15 minutes.

Remove the peel from the mixture and discard. Pour into shallow ramekins or espresso cups. Place in a bain-marie, with the water level halfway up the ramekins, and into the preheated oven for 20 minutes.

Remove from the oven and allow to cool to room temperature. Place in the refrigerator until needed. Just before serving, sprinkle the top with a thin layer of white sugar and use a blowtorch to caramelise the top until golden brown.

Naartjie crème brûlée

NAARTJIE, CRANBERRY AND CHOCOLATE MUFFINS

(v) | MAKES *12* | DIFFICULTY *quick and easy* | PREPARATION TIME *45 minutes*

260 g all-purpose flour
2 tsp baking powder
½ tsp bicarbonate of soda
110 g caster sugar
zest of 3 naartjies, finely grated
45 g milk chocolate, chopped
   into smaller pieces
160 g cranberries
80 ml vegetable oil
250 ml buttermilk
1 egg
130 g icing sugar
naartjie juice
naartjie wedges to serve

Preheat the oven to 180 °C.

Sift the flour, baking powder and bicarbonate of soda into a mixing bowl and add the caster sugar. Add the zest, chocolate and cranberries and mix well. Combine the oil, buttermilk and egg and add to the dry ingredients. Mix until combined.

Use paper cups to line a muffin tray. Spoon the mixture into the cups, about three-quarters of the way to the top.

Bake for 30 minutes. Remove from the oven and allow to cool on a cooling rack.

Mix the icing sugar with just enough naartjie juice to form a stiff icing. When the muffins have cooled completely, drizzle them with the icing and decorate each with a single naartjie wedge.

Naartjie, cranberry and chocolate muffins

CREAMY BAKED ASPARAGUS

(V) | (GF) | (LC) | SERVES *4* | DIFFICULTY *quick and easy* | PREPARATION TIME *35 minutes*

12 thick fresh green asparagus
   spears
200 ml fresh cream
50 ml dry white wine
1 egg
50 g pecorino, grated
2 tbsp parsley, chopped
1 tsp cornflour (Maizena)
salt and freshly milled pepper
   to season
nutmeg, freshly ground

Preheat the oven to 190 °C.

Wash the asparagus well and pat dry. Pack them lying flat in an oven dish. Combine the cream, wine, egg, pecorino, parsley and cornflour. Season with salt, pepper and nutmeg. Pour the mixture over the asparagus.

Bake for 30 minutes or until golden brown.

CHILLED ASPARAGUS, BLUE CHEESE AND BILTONG SOUP

(GF) | (LC) | SERVES *4* | DIFFICULTY *easy* | PREPARATION TIME *40 minutes*

12 asparagus spears
375 ml vegetable stock
olive oil to sauté
2 baby leeks, thinly sliced
250 ml fresh cream
60 g creamy blue cheese
50 g biltong powder
3 tbsp lemon juice, freshly
   squeezed
pink peppercorns, freshly milled
lemon zest

COOK'S TIP: Top with chunky toasted bread crumbs and serve. To make the bread crumbs, use a day-old ciabatta and remove the insides. Break into rough pieces, place in a preheated oven at 180 °C and allow to brown.

Steam the asparagus for a few minutes until al dente. The timing depends on their thickness. Add to the stock, place in a food processor and process until smooth.

Heat the oil in a saucepan and sauté the leeks until they are transparent. Place the asparagus mixture in the saucepan and cook for about 5 minutes on high.

Add the cream and blue cheese and allow to simmer for 25 minutes. Fold in the biltong powder and set aside to cool. Just before serving, add the lemon juice, and sprinkle the milled pink peppercorns and lemon zest on top.

Chilled asparagus, blue cheese and biltong soup

TEMPURA ASPARAGUS SALAD WITH BUTTERNUT AND BABY LETTUCE LEAVES

(v) | SERVES *4* | DIFFICULTY *easy* | PREPARATION TIME *1 hour (including 30 minutes' resting time)*

1 small whole butternut, peeled
  and cut into bite-sized pieces
drizzle of good-quality olive oil
Maldon salt
24 small fresh green asparagus
  spears
2 whole eggs, beaten
130 g all-purpose flour
vegetable oil for deep-frying
140 g baby lettuce leaves
crema di balsamico (balsamic
  reduction)

COOK'S NOTE: The flavour of the asparagus is nutty and the mouth-feel is crispy on the outside and velvety inside.

Preheat the oven to 180°C.

Place the butternut on an oven tray and drizzle with the olive oil. Sprinkle with Maldon salt and bake for 20 minutes or until soft and just turning brown. Remove from the oven and set aside.

Wash the asparagus well and pat them dry. When completely dry, dip them in the egg and then coat them with flour. Set aside to rest for about 30 minutes.

Heat the oil in a saucepan until very hot and deep-fry the asparagus until golden brown. Place on paper towel to drain. On a platter, toss the baby lettuce leaves in olive oil. Top with the butternut and the asparagus. Drizzle with *crema di balsamico* and serve.

Tempura asparagus salad with butternut and baby lettuce leaves

ASPARAGUS AND PECORINO RISOTTO

(GF) | SERVES *4 to 6 as a starter* | DIFFICULTY *moderate* | PREPARATION TIME *about 45 minutes*

500 ml chicken stock
12 asparagus spears
2 tbsp extra-virgin olive oil
1 large leek, finely sliced
4 small cloves garlic, crushed
200 g Arborio rice
125 ml white wine
65 g pecorino cheese, finely
  grated
salt and freshly ground black
  pepper to taste
extra-virgin olive oil to drizzle
extra cheese to serve

COOK'S NOTE: If you are using granulated stock, prepare it according to directions on the container. I, however, prefer to use liquid stock and will use ready-made stock or make my own by covering the carcass of a roast chicken with water, adding a few bay leaves, some whole black peppercorns, an onion (quartered) and a bunch of parsley. I allow this to simmer for hours in order to extract the flavour from the chicken bones. I strain the liquid through a muslin cloth and freeze in 250 ml portions.

Prepare the stock (see cook's note) and blanch the asparagus. They should be al dente.

Place a quarter of the stock and the bottom halves of the asparagus in a food processor and purée. Keep 2 tips per person intact for serving.

Heat the olive oil in a heavy-bottomed pan. Add the leek and garlic and sauté until transparent. Add the rice and cook for about 3 minutes, stirring until the grains are well coated with the oil. Pour in the wine and cook slowly, stirring continuously, until all the wine has been absorbed.

Ladle in the chicken stock, 1 ladle at a time, stirring until the stock is absorbed by the rice. Continue the process until the rice is al dente. A perfect risotto forms a wave when it is done – in other words, it is not too runny and not too dry. Mix in the asparagus and cheese and season.

Drizzle with olive oil and extra cheese, and serve with 2 spears on each plate.

Asparagus and pecorino risotto

SPICY CARROTS WITH HARISSA YOGHURT

(V) | (GF) | (LC) | SERVES *4 to 6* | DIFFICULTY *moderate* | PREPARATION TIME *25 minutes*

250 g baby carrots, peeled and
    tops left on
1 tbsp yellow sugar
1 tsp hot English mustard
    powder
1 tsp smoked Spanish paprika
1 tsp ground cumin
½ tsp ground coriander
4 tbsp vegetable oil
salt and milled black pepper
125 ml natural Greek-style
    yoghurt
1 tbsp harissa paste
½ tsp lemon zest, finely grated
    (and extra for serving)

Steam the carrots for about 10 minutes, then drain and cool under cold running water. Pat them dry.

Mix the sugar, mustard, paprika, cumin and coriander in a small bowl. Toss the carrots in 1 tbsp of the oil, add the spice mixture, salt and pepper and toss to coat the carrots.

Heat the remaining 3 tbsp of oil in a large skillet, and cook the carrots until they have browned – about 5 minutes.

In the meanwhile, place the yoghurt in a small bowl and season with salt and pepper. Add the harissa paste and lemon zest and gently swirl the ingredients around to create a marbled pattern in the yoghurt.

Serve the carrots on a platter with the yoghurt and more lemon zest as an accompaniment to a pilaf or a meat dish.

CARROT, OLIVE AND NASTURTIUM SALAD

(V) | (GF) | (LC) | SERVES *4* | DIFFICULTY *quick and easy* | PREPARATION TIME *15 minutes*

4 medium-sized carrots, peeled
30 g Italian parsley, roughly
    chopped
1 tbsp dill, finely chopped
100 g Calamata olives, pitted
    and roughly chopped
25 g sundried cranberries
handful of nasturtium flowers
1 clove garlic, peeled and crushed
salt and black pepper to season
olive oil

Using a potato peeler, make ribbons from the 4 carrots and place in a bowl. Add the herbs, olives, cranberries, nasturtium flowers and garlic and season with salt and pepper.

Drizzle with enough olive oil to 'moisten' the salad, then toss and serve.

COOK'S TIP: You can prepare this salad 1 hour in advance and allow to stand.

Carrot, olive and nasturtium salad

CARROT SFORMATO

(v) | (LC) | SERVES 6 | DIFFICULTY *a little complex* | PREPARATION TIME *50 to 60 minutes*

400 g carrots, peeled and cut
  into chunks
20 g butter, melted, for greasing
  the moulds
25 g Parmesan, finely grated, for
  coating the moulds
250 ml milk
1 bay leaf
¼ seed of nutmeg, freshly grated
salt and white pepper to taste
25 g butter
20 g all-purpose flour
20 g Parmesan, finely grated
2 egg whites, beaten to form
  soft peaks

COOK'S NOTE: Use dariole moulds or
small tea cups.

Preheat the oven to 180 °C.

Steam the carrots until soft, about 20 to 25 minutes. Drain all excess liquid and place in a bowl. Using a stick blender, purée the carrots and set aside.

Cut out 6 little circles of baking paper. Prepare the moulds by greasing them and placing the paper rounds in the bottom of each. Brush the paper rounds with butter too, and then coat the moulds with the finely grated Parmesan.

Prepare a béchamel sauce by heating the milk in a saucepan, together with the bay leaf, nutmeg, salt and pepper. Melt the butter in another smaller pan, and stir in the flour. Cook for a few minutes, stirring constantly. When the milk is about to reach boiling point, whisk the flour mixture into the milk, and allow the mixture to thicken. Remove from the heat and set aside – cover the surface of the sauce with cling film to prevent a skin from forming.

Add the puréed carrots and the Parmesan to the béchamel and stir well to combine. Fold the beaten egg whites into the mixture and pour into the moulds.

Bake for 20 minutes. Remove from the oven and turn out the moulds by running a knife around the edges and inverting them onto a serving dish. Remove the baking paper rounds.

Serve with a cheese sauce as a starter or a light vegetarian meal, or as an accompaniment to a meat dish.

Carrot sformato

CARROT, PEAR AND GINGER CHUTNEY

(V) | (GF) | MAKES *1250 ml* | DIFFICULTY *moderate* | PREPARATION TIME *1½ hours*

4 medium-sized pears, peeled,
  cored and diced
2 onions, finely diced
120 g sultanas
1 stick cinnamon
1 tbsp fresh ginger, peeled and
  finely grated
1 tsp black mustard seeds
375 ml apple cider vinegar
240 g treacle sugar
1 tsp salt
5 medium-sized carrots, peeled
  and coarsely grated

COOK'S NOTE: If sterilised, sealed and
stored properly, chutney can last up to
12 months. Refrigerate after opening.

Place all the ingredients, except the carrots, in a saucepan and bring to the boil, stirring until the sugar dissolves. Turn the heat down and simmer on medium for 30 minutes.

Sterilise the jars, to protect your preserves, by washing them in hot, soapy water, then rinsing them well, and placing them in a preheated oven at 160 °C for 20 minutes.

Add the carrots and reduce the heat to low – simmer for another 30 minutes until the liquid has reduced and the mixture has thickened. Remove the stick of cinnamon. Ladle the hot chutney into the jars and seal well while hot. Store in a cool, dark place for at least 2 weeks, for the flavours to mature, before eating.

Serve with a strong cheese and a crusty loaf, or with smoked pork.

Carrot, pear and ginger chutney

BANANA AND PEANUT BUTTER BREAKFAST SMOOTHIE

(V) | (GF) | MAKES *2* | DIFFICULTY *quick and easy* | PREPARATION TIME *10 minutes*

2 bananas, peeled and frozen
1 tbsp peanut butter
3 to 4 ice cubes
125 ml cold milk
250 ml natural yoghurt
3 tbsp honey

COOK'S TIP: Wrap the peeled bananas in cling wrap before freezing.

Cut the frozen bananas into chunks and purée them in a blender, processing for about 30 seconds. Add the peanut butter, and process again.

Add the ice cubes, and process until some ice cubes are crushed.

Finally, add the milk, yoghurt and honey, process further until smooth and pour into 2 tall glasses.

BANANA LOAF

(V) | MAKES *1 loaf* | DIFFICULTY *easy* | PREPARATION TIME *1½ hours*

125 g butter
225 g sugar
1 tsp vanilla essence
2 eggs
260 g cake flour
2 tsp baking powder
½ tsp salt
4 to 6 ripe bananas

COOK'S TIP: For best results, the riper bananas the better. The flavour just gets better if left for a few days. Store in a tin or airtight container.

Preheat the oven to 180 °C.

Beat the butter and sugar together until light and creamy. Add the vanilla essence. Then add the eggs, 1 at a time, and beat well after each egg.

Sift all the remaining dry ingredients together and add to the mixture. Mash the bananas with a fork and add. Mix everything together well, and pour into a well-greased bread tin.

Bake for 1 hour until a skewer comes out clean. Allow to stand for a few minutes before tipping the loaf out onto a cooling rack. The loaf should have a crack in the top.

Banana loaf

FRIED BANANAS SMOTHERED IN A GINGER-CARAMEL SAUCE

(v) | SERVES *4 to 6* | DIFFICULTY *moderate* | PREPARATION TIME *1½ hours*

BANANAS
4 tbsp bread crumbs
7 tbsp chopped almonds
1 egg
4 to 6 ripe bananas (not
    bruised)
vegetable oil and butter
    for frying

SAUCE
2 tbsp butter
140 g white sugar
3 tbsp ginger, grated
200 ml coconut milk

To prepare the bananas, mix the bread crumbs and chopped almonds. Beat the egg, dip the bananas into the egg and coat with the almond and bread crumb mixture. Set aside for about 20 minutes while you prepare the sauce.

To make the caramel sauce, melt the butter and sugar in a saucepan. Allow to caramelise slowly – it will go brown and hard, but will melt again when the fluids are added. Add the grated ginger and coconut milk. Bring to the boil, stirring until the mixture is slightly thickened. Set aside until ready to serve. This sauce is served warm.

Heat a mixture of oil and butter in a frying pan and fry the bananas until golden brown on all sides. Serve hot, smothered in the sauce, with a scoop of vanilla ice cream.

BANANA TRIFLE WITH MASCARPONE AND RUM

(v) | SERVES *6 to 8* | DIFFICULTY *quick and easy* | PREPARATION TIME *30 to 40 minutes*

500 g mascarpone
75 g icing sugar
6 tbsp full-cream milk
6 tbsp dark rum
150 g Boudoir biscuits (lady's
    finger biscuits)
2 bananas
2 tbsp lemon juice
4 to 6 ready-made meringues
200 ml whipping cream
1 tbsp cocoa powder for dusting

Beat together mascarpone, icing sugar, half the milk and half the rum. Cover and refrigerate.

Mix together the remaining rum and milk and dip the biscuits into the mixture. Place the biscuits at the bottom of a serving dish.

Slice the bananas and soak in the lemon juice. Crumble half the meringues and fold into the mascarpone mixture. Then fold in the bananas. Spread on top of the finger biscuits. When ready to serve, whip the cream and spread over the top. Place the remaining crumbled meringue on top and dust with cocoa powder.

Fried bananas smothered in a ginger-caramel sauce

DEEP-FRIED PANKO AVOCADO WEDGES

Ⓥ | SERVES 6 | DIFFICULTY *quick and easy* | PREPARATION TIME *about 30 to 40 minutes*

canola oil for frying

33 g all-purpose flour

¼ tsp sea salt

2 large eggs, beaten

125 g panko crumbs (Japanese
  bread crumbs)

2 firm but ripe avocados, pips
  removed, peeled and sliced
  into 4 to 8 wedges

COOK'S NOTE: These make a wonderful
accompaniment to lamb chops, chicken,
steaks or pan-fried fish.

In a saucepan, heat enough oil for deep-frying – the oil must
be smoking hot. I prefer to heat the oil slowly on a medium
heat until ready.

In the meantime, mix the flour and salt in a shallow plate.
Place the beaten eggs and panko crumbs in 2 different
shallow plates.

Dip each avocado wedge into the flour mixture and shake
off excess flour. Next, dip into the egg and then into the
panko crumbs to coat. Set aside in a single layer for a few
minutes. Fry a few slices at a time until golden brown,
making sure not to overcrowd the saucepan. Transfer onto a
plate lined with a few layers of paper towel to absorb the oil.

Serve as soon as you are done, with some Maldon salt on
the side.

Deep-fried panko avocado wedges

AVOCADO AND LIME MOUSSE

(v) | SERVES *4* | DIFFICULTY *a little complex* | PREPARATION TIME *30 minutes (plus 2 hours to set)*

2 large avocados, ripe but not
   bruised
juice and zest of 1 lime
100 g low-fat cream cheese
1 pinch of salt
1 pinch of black pepper, freshly
   milled
2 tsp powdered gelatine (with
   2 tsp water)
1 egg white

Cook's Tip: This mousse can be prepared up to 12 hours in advance, but to
prevent the avocado from turning brown,
place a layer of cling film over the top and
press it gently onto the surface of the
mousse. Keep chilled until needed.

Halve the avocados and remove the pips. Scoop the flesh into a small bowl, add the lime zest and juice, and blend until very smooth using a stick blender.

Beat in the cream cheese and season with salt and pepper. Place the water in a small heatproof bowl and sprinkle the gelatine over it. Leave for 1 minute to go spongy. Then place the bowl in a pan of hot water and stir until the gelatine dissolves.

Whisk the egg white in a large bowl until standing in soft peaks. This will give the mousse a light texture. Drizzle the dissolved gelatine over the avocado mixture and stir until well combined. Add the egg white and carefully fold it into the mixture.

Spoon into ramekin dishes or glasses and cover with cling film – refrigerate for 2 hours, or until set.

AVOCADO LASSI

(v) | (GF) | (LC) | MAKES *2 tall glasses* | DIFFICULTY *quick and easy* | PREPARATION TIME *15 minutes*

1 ripe avocado
250 ml Bulgarian yoghurt
3 tbsp honey
1 tsp lime juice
250 ml milk
generous pinch of salt
handful of pistachios
raspberries to serve

Place the avocado, yoghurt, honey, lime juice, milk and salt in a bowl and blend, using a stick blender, until smooth.

Once blended, pour the lassi into glasses and top with the pistachios and raspberries. Serve.

Cook's Note: A lassi is a popular yoghurt-based drink originating in India and Pakistan. It can be either savoury or sweet. This is a healthy substitute for a meal.

Avocado lassi

RICE WRAPS WITH AVOCADO

(v) | SERVES *4* | DIFFICULTY *quick and easy* | PREPARATION TIME *20 minutes*

8 Vietnamese rice wraps
hot water for dipping
1 avocado, pip and skin
  removed and cut into thin
  slices
1 carrot, peeled and julienned
4 spring onions, cut lengthwise
  into thin strips
soy sauce for dipping
sweet chilli sauce for dipping

Dip the rice wraps into the hot water to soften them, and lay on a clean flat surface. Place the avocado, julienned carrots and spring onion towards the top middle of the wrap. Fold the bottom half over and roll from one side so that you have a firm roll. Cut the tops off to expose the filling.

Serve with soy sauce and sweet chilli sauce for dipping.

Rice wraps with avocado

PRESERVED LEMONS

(V) | (GF) | (LC) | MAKES *500 ml* | DIFFICULTY *quick and easy* | PREPARATION TIME *30 minutes*

3 to 4 small, unwaxed lemons
75 g salt
fresh lemon juice (enough to
   fill a jar)

Cut the lemons into quarters, leaving the quarters attached at the stalk end. Sprinkle as much salt as you can into the cuts, and squeeze the quarters back into shape. Place in a 500-ml jar, stalk end down, packing them tightly.

Sprinkle the rest of the salt over, seal and leave for 4 to 5 days, giving the jar a shake every now and then until they have produced quite a lot of juice.

Top up the jar with lemon juice so that the lemons are completely covered. Reseal and leave for about 2 weeks before using.

See cover image.

CITRUS LEMONADE

(V) | (GF) | MAKES *500 ml (2½ litres of the mixed drink)* | DIFFICULTY *quick and easy*
PREPARATION TIME *30 to 45 minutes*

225 g white sugar
juice of 6 lemons
juice of 1 ruby grapefruit
juice of 2 oranges
250 ml water
2 litres cold sparkling water
1 lime, sliced into rounds
mint sprigs to serve

Pour the sugar, lemon juice, grapefruit juice and orange juice into a small pot and add the water. Bring to the boil, stirring continuously, until the sugar dissolves. Set aside to cool. When cool, refrigerate until icy cold.

When ready to use, mix the syrup with the cold sparkling water, add a few ice cubes, the slices of lime and a few sprigs of mint.

Citrus lemonade

LEMON AND YOGHURT CAKE WITH ORANGE AND CARDAMOM SYRUP

(v) | MAKES *1 x 20 cm cake* | DIFFICULTY *easy* | PREPARATION TIME *1½ hours*

CAKE
4 tbsp desiccated coconut
250 g butter, softened
4 tbsp lemon zest, finely grated
250 g caster sugar
3 eggs
50 g ground almonds
juice of 1 lemon
400 g self-raising flour
250 g Greek-style yoghurt (plus
   extra to serve)

SYRUP
zest of 1 orange
juice of 1 orange
125 ml water
100 ml honey
5 cardamom pods, bruised

Preheat the oven to 180 °C and grease a 20-cm ring-cake tin. Toast the coconut by dry-roasting in a pan over a medium heat until golden brown. Set aside to cool.

To make the cake, use an electric beater to beat the butter, zest and sugar until light and fluffy. Add the eggs 1 at a time, beating well after each addition.

With a wooden spoon, stir in the coconut, almonds, lemon juice, flour and yoghurt until just combined. Spoon the mixture into the prepared cake tin and spread evenly. Bake for about 50 minutes, remove from oven and allow to stand for 5 minutes before removing the cake from the tin.

While the cake is in the oven, combine all the ingredients for the syrup in a pot and stir until it begins to boil. Reduce the heat and simmer until slightly reduced.

Remove the cake from the tin and place on a serving dish. Remove and discard the cardamom from the syrup. Pour the syrup over the cake while still hot.

Serve with a blob of thick Greek-style yoghurt.

Lemon and yoghurt cake with orange and cardamom syrup

LEMON PANNA COTTA ON A SWEET BASIL PESTO

MAKES *6* | DIFFICULTY *a little complex* | PREPARATION TIME *1½ hours (plus about 2 hours' setting time)*

PANNA COTTA
300 ml full-cream milk
300 ml cream
100 g caster sugar
thumb-length strip of lemon
    zest, pith removed
1½ tsp gelatine powder
1 tbsp tepid water
4 tbsp fresh lemon juice

PESTO
50 g diced almonds
100 g fresh basil, stalks removed
80 ml olive oil
1 tbsp lemon juice, freshly
    squeezed
2 tsp caramelised verjuice syrup
1 tsp vanilla paste
1 tbsp honey
pinch of freshly milled black
    pepper

For the panna cotta, place the milk, cream and caster sugar into a saucepan with the strip of lemon zest, over a medium heat. Bring very gently up to just below boiling point, stirring now and then to help the sugar dissolve. Remove from the heat and set aside for 10 minutes to allow the flavour of the lemon to infuse.

In the meanwhile, sprinkle the gelatine over the water in a small bowl and set aside to sponge for 5 minutes. Place the bowl in a pan of simmering water – so the water reaches halfway up the sides – and leave until the gelatine becomes clear. Remove and allow to cool for 1 minute.

Stir the gelatine into the creamy milk mixture and discard the lemon zest. Strain the mixture into a clean bowl. Stir in the lemon juice.

Pour the mixture into 6 lightly oiled dariole moulds. Allow to cool for another 20 minutes before refrigerating for about 2 hours, or until set.

To make the pesto, place the diced almonds in a pan and dry-roast over a medium heat. Set aside to cool.

Place the basil, oil, lemon juice and verjuice syrup in a jug and blend with a stick blender. Add the vanilla paste, honey, black pepper and roasted nuts and mix well. Refrigerate in an airtight container until needed – for up to 1 week.

Remove the panna cotta from the fridge. Fill a shallow bowl with hot water and dip each mould in the water for 30 seconds. Use a sharp knife tip to loosen the sides of the panna cotta and release the vacuum. Place each little mould face down onto flat serving plates and serve with pesto.

Lemon panna cotta on a sweet basil pesto

SUMMER

— · —

WATERMELONS 46 | TOMATOES 50

FIGS 56 | MANGOES 64 | GRANADILLAS 70

STRAWBERRIES 76 | PINEAPPLES 82

— · —

Our vegetable patch and fruit trees proved

that Mother Nature knew that we preferred

the refreshing taste of chilled watermelon

slices, crispy salads and sun-ripened figs during

summertime. The fig tree dropped ripe figs

oozing with syrup and I had to fight the bees and

the birds to get to them first.

Watermelon granita (recipe on page 46)

WATERMELON GRANITA

V | GF | LC | MAKES *about 1 litre* | DIFFICULTY *quick and easy*
PREPARATION TIME *about 2 hours (including freezing time)*

1 litre watermelon juice, pips
   removed and liquidised using
   a stick blender

Strain the watermelon juice through a sieve, and then pour into a shallow dish and place in the freezer. Leave for 1 hour before stirring and breaking up the ice crystals every 20 to 30 minutes until the crystals are small and flaky.

Serve with a sprig of mint as a palate cleanser or simply in a bowl on a hot summer's day.

See image on page 45.

WATERMELON AND CHORIZO SALAD

LC | SERVES *8* | DIFFICULTY *quick and easy* | PREPARATION TIME *20 minutes*

2 tbsp good-quality olive oil
225 g chorizo, cut into slices
¼ small ripe watermelon, pips
   removed and cut into shavings
½ red onion, sliced very thin
fresh basil, finely shredded

Heat the olive oil in a pan and flash-fry the chorizo. Retain the oil to use as a dressing. Set aside to cool.

Place the watermelon shavings onto a platter and top with the red onion. Add the chorizo and basil and drizzle with the cold olive oil from the pan.

Serve with a cheese platter as a light lunch or as an accompaniment to pork belly.

Watermelon and chorizo salad

WATERMELON JAM

(v) | (GF) | MAKES *4 x 250g jars* | DIFFICULTY *moderate* | PREPARATION TIME *about 1½ hours*

3 tbsp powdered pectin
1½ litres watermelon juice, pips removed and sieved, retaining the pulp
1 kg sugar
7 tbsp lemon juice, freshly squeezed and strained (place the pips in a muslin cloth and tie with string)

Mix the pectin into the watermelon juice. Pour the juice into a heavy-bottomed saucepan and add the sugar, lemon juice and the muslin bag with pips. Gently bring to the boil.

When the mixture is boiling, turn the heat down and simmer to reduce the liquid to about half.

Add the watermelon pulp and continue simmering until the correct consistency.

Remove the muslin bag. Pour the hot jam into hot sterilised jars and seal immediately.

COOK'S TIP: To test the consistency of the mixture, drop a spoonful of jam onto a cold saucer and pull your finger down the middle – the 2 halves should not merge.

A quick and easy way to sterilise jars is to place them, without lids, for 3 minutes in a microwave on high.

The jam is a perfect accompaniment to venison. It can be stored for a year or more if kept out of direct sunlight. When opened, keep in the refrigerator.

Watermelon jam

TOMATO TART

SERVES *10 to 12 as a light meal or starter* | DIFFICULTY *a little complex*
PREPARATION TIME *about 1½ hours (plus 2 hours for the pastry to rest)*

PASTRY
125 g unsalted butter
250 g all-purpose flour
1½ tsp salt
3 tbsp cold water
1 medium egg yolk

FILLING
6 to 8 medium ripe tomatoes
salt and pepper to taste
3 tbsp olive oil
500 g onions, finely chopped
250 g smoked bacon, diced
1 tsp caster sugar
3 cloves garlic, peeled and
    crushed
2 x 400 g canned peeled
    tomatoes, drained
3 tsp tomato paste
2 medium eggs
2 tsp fresh oregano, roughly
    chopped
60 g mature Gruyère, grated

COOK'S NOTE: The pastry can be kept
2 to 3 days in the refrigerator, or for up
to a month in the freezer. Allow plenty
of time for the dough to return to the
temperature of a 'cool place' before using.

To make the pastry, place the butter in a small bowl and beat well with a spatula until very soft and creamy. Sift the flour onto a work surface and make a well. Add the salt and water to the well and mix it into the flour using your fingertips. Add the egg yolk and softened butter and work together with your fingertips to form a soft dough. Knead very lightly before forming a ball. Line a clean dishcloth with flour and wrap the pastry in the cloth. Rest in a cool place for at least 2 hours or overnight.

Preheat the oven to 180 °C.

Roll out the pastry on a lightly floured surface and lift onto a 30-cm loose-bottomed tart tin. Press the pastry down without stretching it too much. Prick the bottom with a fork and bake blind for 15 minutes. Then remove from the oven and allow to cool. Turn the oven temperature up to 200 °C.

To make the filling, cut a cross in the bottom of the tomatoes using a small, sharp knife. Cover them with boiling water and leave for 10 to 15 minutes. The skin should slide off easily. Discard the skin and cut the tomatoes into slices. Sprinkle them with salt and allow them to drain in a colander.

In a saucepan, heat the olive oil and add the onions and bacon. Cook over a moderate heat for about 15 minutes, stirring frequently, until the onions are soft and golden. Add the sugar, garlic, canned tomatoes and tomato paste, and simmer for 10 minutes until slightly reduced. Stir occasionally. Remove the saucepan from the heat and allow to cool a little.

Continued on page 52

Tomato tart

Continued from page 50

Whisk the eggs lightly in a bowl, season with salt and pepper and add the oregano. Stir this into the tomato mixture. Spread the filling in the pastry case. Arrange the drained tomato slices neatly on top and sprinkle with the grated Gruyère. Bake for 30 minutes.

Remove from the oven and allow to cool for a few minutes before serving. Serve with a garden salad as a light meal, or on its own as a starter.

CHILLED TOMATO AND FRESH GINGER SOUP

(V) | (GF) | (LC) | SERVES *2 to 4 (about 400 ml)* | DIFFICULTY *easy* | PREPARATION TIME *1½ hours*

6 Roma tomatoes, halved and
  pips removed
30 ml olive oil for roasting
Maldon salt and freshly milled
  black pepper to season
½ tbsp sugar
3 sprigs French tarragon
¼ tsp fresh ginger, peeled and
  coarsely chopped
125 ml tomato juice
1 tbsp good-quality olive oil
1 tsp lemon juice, freshly
  squeezed

Preheat the oven to 180 °C.

Place the tomatoes in a roasting dish and drizzle with the olive oil. Season with salt and pepper, and sprinkle some sugar in each of the tomatoes. Add the sprigs of tarragon and roast for about 1 hour, turning them after 45 minutes. Set aside to cool.

Place the ginger and the tomato juice, together with the tomatoes and tarragon (stalks removed) from the roasting pan, in a blender and blend until smooth. Add the olive oil and lemon juice.

Pour into a container, cover and chill, preferably overnight.

COOK'S NOTE: Add a shot of vodka for something different. Add a little cold water to dilute if the consistency is too thick when serving.

Chilled tomato and fresh ginger soup

PLUMP TOMATOES STUFFED WITH
TOASTED BREAD CRUMBS, GARLIC AND ANCHOVY

SERVES *4* | DIFFICULTY *easy* | PREPARATION TIME *about 1 hour*

4 large ripe tomatoes
50 g toasted bread crumbs
4 tbsp salted butter, melted
4 anchovy fillets, finely chopped
2 tbsp Italian parsley, chopped
1 large clove garlic, crushed
¼ tsp preserved lemons (see
   page 38), finely chopped
black pepper, freshly milled
olive oil to drizzle

Preheat the oven to 180 °C.

Cut the tops off the tomatoes and remove the inner flesh and pips. Discard the pips, but retain the tomato 'lids' and flesh. Mix the bread crumbs, melted butter, anchovy, parsley, garlic, preserved lemons and the inside flesh of the tomatoes. Season with black pepper.

Stuff each tomato firmly, then place the 'lids' back on top. Place the tomatoes in an oven dish and drizzle with olive oil. Roast for about 30 to 40 minutes. Serve hot or at room temperature.

MEDITERRANEAN TOMATO BUNNY CIAO

(v) | SERVES *6* | DIFFICULTY *quick and easy* | PREPARATION TIME *45 minutes*

250 g vine tomatoes
olive oil
Maldon salt
1 boule
80 g basil pesto
1 ball buffalo mozzarella
black pepper, freshly milled
fresh basil to serve

COOK'S NOTE: A boule, from the French for a ball, is a rustic French loaf, round in shape. It is because of this specific loaf that a bread baker in France is called a *boulanger* and the place where you buy bread, the *boulangerie*.

Preheat the oven to 180 °C.

Place the vine tomatoes in a roasting pan and drizzle with olive oil. Sprinkle with Maldon salt and roast for about 30 minutes. Set aside to cool slightly.

Cut the top off the boule and hollow out.

Spread the pesto on the bottom of the hollowed-out boule. Fill with the roasted vine tomatoes. Tear the buffalo mozzarella into smaller pieces and add to the tomatoes in the boule.

Sprinkle with freshly milled black pepper. Add a couple of fresh basil leaves. Drizzle with olive oil and serve.

Mediterranean tomato bunny ciao

ARANCINI WITH FIG AND CANDIED PISTACHIOS

(v) | MAKES *8 golf ball-sized arancini* | DIFFICULTY *a little complex* | PREPARATION TIME *1¼ hours*

PISTACHIOS
1 tbsp butter
60 g pistachios
1 tbsp honey

RISOTTO
1 tbsp olive oil
1 small onion, chopped
200 g Arborio rice
190 ml white wine
500 ml vegetable stock
60 g Parmesan, finely grated
1 tbsp butter

FOR FRYING
8 small figs, peeled
2 tsp cream cheese
1 egg, beaten
185 g couscous, uncooked
canola oil for deep-frying

To make the candied pistachios, melt the butter and fry the pistachios lightly. Add the honey and allow to bubble for 3 to 5 minutes. Pour onto an oven tray and allow to cool.

Prepare the risotto by heating the olive oil in a saucepan and frying the onion on a medium heat until transparent. Add the rice and fry for 2 to 3 minutes. Add the wine and cook until all the liquid has been absorbed. Ladle the stock into the risotto, making sure that every spoonful gets absorbed before you add the next. The rice should be al dente within 20 to 30 minutes.

Remove from the heat, add the Parmesan and the butter, stir and leave to cool.

Stuff each fig with a quarter teaspoon of cream cheese and 2 pistachios. When the rice has cooled, divide it up into 8 portions. Roll a ball in your hands and press it flat onto your palm. Place a stuffed fig onto the rice and roll into a ball about the size of a golf ball.

Dip the balls into the beaten egg and then into the couscous. Heat the oil in a saucepan, and when hot, drop the arancini into the oil. Deep-fry until golden brown, drain on paper towel and serve immediately.

COOK'S NOTE: Arancini are Sicilian rice balls, made golden with saffron and traditionally stuffed with a ragù (meat sauce), cheese or peas. They are then rolled in crumbs and fried. The name is derived from the Italian word for 'little orange' (arancino) because of their colour and shape. In the rest of Italy it is an innovative way of getting rid of leftover risotto.

If you cannot find small figs, then use half a fig instead of a whole. These are a great accompaniment to a cheese board.

Arancini with fig and candied pistachios

FIG MILLE-FEUILLE

(v) | SERVES *4* | DIFFICULTY *a little complex* | PREPARATION TIME *about 1 hour*

250 g ready-made puff pastry
500 ml milk (plus 60 ml extra)
1 heaped tbsp custard powder
2 tbsp yellow sugar
1 tsp rosewater
2 egg whites
1 tsp caster sugar
4 to 6 fresh figs

COOK'S TIP: In French *mille-feuille* means 'a thousand leaves'.

To prevent a 'skin' forming on the custard, place cling film on the surface of the custard while it's cooling.

Preheat the oven to 200 °C.

Cut the cold pastry into rectangles of about 6 cm x 2½ cm and place onto an oven tray lined with baking paper. Bake for 12 to 15 minutes until puffed and golden brown. Remove from the oven and set aside.

To prepare the custard, scald the milk. Then mix the custard powder into the extra 60 ml milk. Add the sugar and the custard mixture to the scalded milk and stir continuously to prevent lumps from forming. Use a whisk to ensure a smooth custard. Stir over a low heat for another 5 minutes until the custard has thickened. Add the rosewater and set aside to cool.

Beat the egg whites and caster sugar together until stiff peaks form. Fold into the cooled custard. Decant the mixture into a metal bowl and place over a double boiler. Stir gently until the custard is light, fluffy and thick. Allow to cool.

Cut the figs into slices. To assemble the mille-feuille, carefully separate each pastry rectangle into 3 parts. Place the bottom flat part on a plate, top with some of the custard and 3 slices of figs, and repeat with the middle section. Top with the puffed-up golden-brown sheet of pastry. Serve.

Fig mille-feuille

SEARED FILLET WITH COFFEE, CARDAMOM AND FIGS

(GF) | SERVES *4* | DIFFICULTY *quick and easy* | PREPARATION TIME *30 minutes*

500 ml strong filter coffee
4 tsp sugar
seeds from 2 cardamom pods,
　　dry-roasted in a pan and
　　ground in a mortar and pestle
4 fresh Adam's figs
4 thick-cut fillet medallions
olive oil for searing
salt to season

Dissolve the sugar in the coffee. Pour into a pan, add the cardamom and reduce to half. Cut the figs into slices to make flat discs, about 4 per fig, and place into the coffee mixture. Allow to cook for 3 minutes and set aside.

Heat a heavy-bottomed skillet until very hot. Rub the fillet medallions with a little olive oil. Sear on all sides until brown. Remove from the heat and season with the salt.

Serve topped with the figs-and-coffee mixture.

Seared fillet with coffee, cardamom and figs

EAT 'N MESS

(v) | SERVES *6 to 8* | DIFFICULTY *moderate* | PREPARATION TIME *about 2½ hours*

MERINGUE
22 cream crackers
1 cup hazelnuts, toasted and
   roughly chopped
4 egg whites
pinch of cream of tartar
215 g caster sugar
1 tsp vanilla essence

FILLING
250 ml cream
generous pinch of caster sugar
8 to 10 fresh figs, quartered
twist of pink peppercorns

Preheat the oven to 140 °C.

Line a Swiss roll pan with baking paper.

Place the crackers in a food processor and blend until they resemble rough crumbs. Transfer to a bowl, add the nuts and mix.

Beat the egg whites with a pinch of cream of tartar to soft peaks. Add the caster sugar, 1 tablespoon at a time, beating constantly until a velvety, glossy meringue forms. Fold in the vanilla essence, followed by the cracker and hazelnut mixture. Spoon onto an oven tray and bake for 1 hour until crisp. Set aside to cool completely.

When the meringue has cooled, make the filling by beating the cream with the caster sugar until stiff.

To assemble, break the meringue into chunks and place on a platter. Add the cream and the figs, and top with a twist of pink peppercorns.

Serve immediately.

Eat 'n mess

LAYERED MANGO AND GRAPE DESSERT

(V) | (GF) | SERVES *4 to 6* | DIFFICULTY *quick and easy* | PREPARATION TIME *30 minutes*

250 ml cream
1 tsp caster sugar
¼ tsp vanilla paste
250 ml full-cream Greek
   yoghurt
250 g seedless red grapes
1 large mango, peeled and cut
   into thin shavings
treacle sugar for sprinkling

Cook's Tip: This dish is equally good
served at breakfast with muesli.

Beat the cream and caster sugar together to form soft peaks. Add the vanilla paste. Fold the Greek yoghurt into the mixture until well blended.

To assemble, cut half of the grapes in half. Place the mango shavings in the bottom of a shallow dish. Top with the halved grapes and a layer of the cream mixture. Top with a generous sprinkling of treacle sugar, evenly spread over the top.

Arrange the rest of the grapes on top, cover with cling film and refrigerate overnight.

PRAWN AND MANGO SALAD

(GF) | (LC) | SERVES *4 as a starter* | DIFFICULTY *quick and easy* | PREPARATION TIME *20 minutes*

6 tbsp olive oil, half for frying
   and the rest for the vinaigrette
12 prawns, with the heads and
   shells intact
1 tsp balsamic vinegar
½ tsp honey
80 g baby lettuce leaves
1 large mango, cut into slices
pomegranate arils

Heat half the oil in a frying pan. Flash-fry the prawns until they just change colour and turn a bright pink. Remove from the heat and allow to cool.

Make the vinaigrette by mixing the remaining olive oil with the balsamic vinegar and honey. Toss the lettuce leaves in the dressing and place on a plate. Place the mango slices on the lettuce and top with the prawns and pomegranate arils.

Prawn and mango salad

MANGO CURD TARTLETS

(v) | MAKES *6 to 8 tartlets or 1 large tart, and about 1½ litres curd* | DIFFICULTY *a little complex*
PREPARATION TIME *2½ hours (plus 2 hours' resting time for pastry)*

CURD
850 g ripe mango, peeled, pitted
  and cubed
195 g sugar
90 ml lime (or lemon) juice
2 pinches of salt
8 large egg yolks
115 g unsalted butter, cut into
  cubes

TARTLETS
125 g unsalted butter
250 g cake flour
½ tsp salt
1 heaped tsp five-spice
2 tbsp caster sugar
3 tbsp water
1 medium-sized egg yolk

FILLING
2 eggs, separated
500 ml mango curd

COOK'S TIP: The pastry dough can be
stored in the refrigerator for up to 3 days
or in the freezer for up to 1 month.

  For a savoury pastry, omit the sugar
and the five-spice, and use 1 tsp salt.

  You can bake the tart bases ahead of
time and store them in an airtight container for 1 to 2 days.

To make the curd, blend the mango, sugar, lime juice and salt in a food processor until smooth. Add the egg yolks and purée for another 15 seconds.

Place the mixture in a medium-sized metal or glass bowl set over a saucepan of gently simmering water. Whisk the purée constantly until it coats the back of a wooden spoon. This will take about 10 to 15 minutes.

Remove from the heat and whisk the butter into the mixture, 1 cube at a time. Allow to cool a little before placing in an airtight container. Refrigerate overnight.

To make the tartlets, place the butter in a small bowl and beat well with a spoon or spatula until soft and creamy. Sift the flour onto a cool work surface. Add the salt, five-spice and sugar to the flour and make a well. Add the water to the well and mix into the flour using your fingertips. Add the softened butter and egg yolk and work the ingredients together using your fingertips to form a soft dough, taking care not to overwork it. Form the dough into a ball and wrap in a clean dishcloth lined with flour. Leave to rest in a cool place for a minimum of 2 hours.

Preheat the oven to 200 °C.

Grease loose-bottomed tart tins with a diameter of 12 cm. Roll out the pastry on a lightly floured surface and lift onto the tins. Press the dough in gently without stretching it too much. Prick the bottom with a fork and bake blind for 15 minutes. Remove from oven and allow to cool. Reduce oven to 180 °C.

Continued on page 68

Mango curd tartlets

Continued from page 66

Beat the egg yolks lightly and add to the curd. Using a hand mixer, beat the egg whites until soft peaks form. Fold into the curd mixture and spoon into the tart bases. Bake for 20 minutes or until golden brown. Top with a strawberry or any other berries and serve at room temperature.

PICKLED OX TONGUE WITH MANGO SALSA IN ASPIC

SERVES *8* | DIFFICULTY *moderate* | PREPARATION TIME *about 3 hours*

TONGUE
1 pickled ox tongue
3 juniper berries
6 black peppercorns, whole
1 carrot, peeled and cut into chunks
1 small onion, peeled and quartered
2 bay leaves
250 ml dry white wine
1 litre water

ASPIC JELLY
210 ml sparkling rosé wine
2 tbsp caster sugar
2 tsp gelatine powder
1½ tsp fresh lime juice

SALSA
1 large mango, cut into small cubes
1 red jalapeno chilli, pips removed and finely sliced
handful of fresh coriander, stems removed

To prepare the tongue, place all the ingredients into a pot and allow to simmer for 2 to 2½ hours until soft. Remove from the water and allow to cool. Remove the skin.

To make the aspic jelly, heat half of the rosé wine and allow to simmer. Whisk in the sugar and gelatine, making sure everything has dissolved before adding the remaining wine and the lime juice. Pour into a jug and allow to cool.

For the salsa, arrange the mango in the bottom of mini loaf tins, and top with the coriander and chilli. Pour the gelatine mixture over the salsa and refrigerate overnight.

To serve, cut the tongue into thin slices. Briefly dip the tin with the jelly into hot water and invert. To loosen the sides, use a sharp knife that has also been dipped into the hot water.

Cut the jelly into chunky slices and serve with a fresh green salad as a light meal.

COOK'S TIP: The tongue is best prepared a day or two in advance and kept in the fridge.

Pickled ox tongue with mango salsa in aspic

BAKED GRANADILLA AND SAGO CUSTARD

(v) | (GF) | SERVES *4 to 6* | DIFFICULTY *easy* | PREPARATION TIME *1¼ hours (plus 1 hour for sago to soak)*

5 tbsp sago
500 ml milk
pulp of 3 granadillas
1 tsp vanilla essence
¼ tsp rosewater
2 eggs
2 tbsp sugar
¼ tsp salt
melted butter for brushing

COOK'S TIP: To check whether cooked through, test with a knife – if the blade comes out clean, the dish is ready.

Preheat the oven to 180 °C.

Soak the sago in half a cup of the milk for 1 hour. Then bring the rest of the milk to the boil and stir the sago mixture into it. Simmer for 5 minutes, stirring continuously. Remove from the heat, stir the granadilla pulp, vanilla essence and rosewater into the mixture and set aside.

Beat the eggs, sugar and salt together until light and creamy. Pour the hot milk mixture over the egg mixture and mix. Brush an oven dish lightly with melted butter. Pour the mixture into the oven dish and place the dish in an oven tray. Fill the tray with warm water to cover the oven dish to halfway up the sides. Bake in the bain-marie for about 45 minutes or until set.

Serve warm.

SEARED NORWEGIAN SALMON WITH FRESH GRANADILLA AND MINT

(GF) | (LC) | SERVES *4* | DIFFICULTY *quick and easy* | PREPARATION TIME *20 minutes*

2 tbsp canola oil
2 x 300 g salmon fillets, skin on
salt to season
pulp of 4 granadillas
bunch of mint, finely chopped

Heat the oil in a skillet until very hot. Place the fillets in the pan, flesh side down, and sear for about 4 minutes before turning them onto the skin. Cook for about another 3 minutes, season with salt and remove from the heat.

Scrape the pulp from the granadillas onto the salmon and top with the mint.

Serve warm or at room temperature with a steamed potato and avocado or, for a carb-free option, with a fresh, green salad.

Seared Norwegian salmon with fresh granadilla and mint

GRANADILLA ÉCLAIRS WITH WHITE CHOCOLATE TOPPING

(v) | MAKES *20* | DIFFICULTY *moderate* | PREPARATION TIME *1½ hours*

CHOUX PASTRY
80 g butter
250 ml water
1 ml salt
120 g cake flour
4 eggs

FILLING
250 ml fresh cream, stiffly
  beaten
10 ml icing sugar

TOPPING
200 g white chocolate, melted
pulp from 3 granadillas

Preheat the oven to 200 °C.

To make the pastry, melt the butter, water and salt in a large saucepan and bring to the boil. Add the flour and beat vigorously until the mixture forms a ball that pulls away from the sides of the pan. Remove from the heat and allow to cool slightly – about 15 minutes.

Transfer the mixture to a bowl and add the eggs, 1 at a time, beating gently after each addition with an electric hand-held beater on a low speed. The mixture should become stiff and shiny and hold its shape.

Using a piping bag, pipe the pastry onto a greased baking tray and bake for 10 minutes. Reduce the heat to 180 °C and bake until the éclairs are golden brown (about another 10 minutes). Remove from the oven and make a small slit in the side of each. Return to the oven to dry out for 1 minute. Allow the éclairs to cool before filling them through the slit.

To make the filling, beat the cream and sugar until the mixture forms soft peaks. Fill a piping bag with the cream and pipe a generous amount into each éclair.

Drizzle the filled éclairs with the melted white chocolate and granadilla pulp, and serve.

Granadilla éclairs with white chocolate topping

CHRISTMAS STRUDEL

(v) | SERVES *10 to 12* | DIFFICULTY *moderate* | PREPARATION TIME *1¼ hours*

3 Granny Smith apples, peeled,
   cored, cubed and tossed in
   lemon juice
25 g butter
1 tbsp brown sugar
300 g Christmas mince meat
75 g glacé red cherries,
   quartered
35 g pecan nuts, roughly
   chopped
25 g almonds, flaked and toasted
   (plus extra for sprinkling)
zest and juice of 1 orange
2 granadillas
150 g bread crumbs, toasted
cake flour for sprinkling
4 sheets phyllo pastry
120 g butter, melted
50 g ground almonds
smooth apricot jam for
   brushing
2 tbsp water
icing sugar to dredge

Preheat the oven to 190 °C.

Place the apples in a pan with the butter and sugar and cook until soft and golden – about 15 minutes. Allow to cool.

Place the cooled apple mixture in a bowl together with the Christmas mince meat, cherries, pecans, almonds, zest and juice, the pulp from 1 of the granadillas, as well as half the bread crumbs and stir well to combine.

Arrange a clean dishcloth on a suitable surface, sprinkle with flour and then layer a sheet of phyllo on top. Brush the phyllo with butter and repeat with the remaining phyllo. Sprinkle the remaining bread crumbs and the ground almonds evenly over the top of the final sheet of buttered phyllo.

Spread the fruit-and-nut filling on the pastry, leaving a 3-cm border all round. Fold the borders on the long sides in over the filling. Start rolling up the pastry by turning in the border along the short edge nearest to you. Then keep rolling, lifting the dishcloth to help form the roll.

Before completing the roll, lift the far edge of the dishcloth over a paper-lined baking tray. Finish rolling the strudel carefully onto the tray, ending with strudel seam side down. Brush all over with more melted butter and sprinkle with flaked almonds. Bake until crisp and golden – about 45 minutes.

Thin the jam with the water and warm slightly in the microwave, together with the pulp from the last granadilla. Remove the strudel from the oven. Brush generously with warm jam and granadilla, and dredge with icing sugar. Sprinkle with the remaining roasted almond flakes. Serve warm with pouring cream.

Christmas strudel

STRAWBERRY AND PINE NUT BARS

(v) | MAKES *12* | DIFFICULTY *moderate* | PREPARATION TIME *1 hour*

200 g all-purpose flour
200 g porridge oats
250 g butter, melted
175 g muscovado sugar
zest of 1 lemon, finely grated
100 g pack pine nuts
250 g strawberries, quartered
sesame seeds to sprinkle

COOK'S NOTE: These will keep for
2 to 3 days.

Preheat the oven to 170 °C.

Butter a shallow 23-cm square tin. Tip the flour, oats and butter into a mixing bowl and use your fingers to work the mixture together to form coarse crumbs. Mix in the sugar, lemon zest and three quarters of the pine nuts using your hands. Press together well to form large sticky clumps.

Drop about two thirds of the oat mixture into the base of the tin, spread it out and press down very lightly – but don't pack it too firmly. Scatter the strawberries on top, sprinkle the rest of the oat mixture over, then the remaining pine nuts and press down lightly. Sprinkle with sesame seeds.

Bake for 35 to 40 minutes until a pale golden colour on top. Cut into 12 bars with a sharp knife while still warm, then leave to cool in the tin before removing.

ROASTED STRAWBERRY CONSERVE

(v) | (GF) | MAKES *500 ml* | DIFFICULTY *quick and easy* | PREPARATION TIME *35 to 40 minutes*

500 g strawberries
340 g sugar
juice of 1 lemon
4 tbsp crème de cassis

Preheat the oven to 220 °C.

Arrange strawberries in a single layer in a roasting pan coated with a non-stick cooking spray. Sprinkle with the sugar and place in the preheated oven. Roast them, stirring 2 to 3 times, for 20 minutes or until the sugar, reduced to a jewel-red syrup, starts to boil.

Add the juice of a lemon to the conserve and allow the mixture to cool for about 15 minutes. Turn into a sterilised, warm jar. Pour over a thin film of crème de cassis and place the lid on securely. Serve with scones and cream.

Roasted strawberry conserve

STRAWBERRY AND FRANGELICO SEMIFREDDO

(v) | (GF) | SERVES *8 to 10* | DIFFICULTY *moderate* | PREPARATION TIME *20 to 30 minutes*

100 g fresh strawberries
85 g caster sugar
280 ml double-thick cream
4 tbsp Frangelico
500 g crème fraîche
fresh strawberries to serve

COOK'S NOTE: The semifreddo can be frozen for up to a month.

Line the base of a ring tin with baking paper.

Mash the strawberries and half the sugar in a bowl with a fork.

Whisk the cream, the remaining sugar and the Frangelico to form soft peaks. Beat the crème fraîche briefly, also to form soft peaks. Gently fold the cream mixture and the crème fraîche together.

Pour the mashed strawberries into the cream and give a few stirs only, just enough to swirl it through the creamy mixture. Pour the mixture into the lined tin and smooth the top.

Place the semifreddo in the freezer, uncovered, until it firms up, and then cover with cling film.

To serve, thaw the semifreddo in the fridge for 1 hour. Turn upside down onto a serving platter and peel off the baking paper. Scatter some fresh strawberries onto the serving platter. Serve in slices.

Strawberry and Frangelico semifreddo

STRAWBERRY FLAN

ⓥ | MAKES *1* | DIFFICULTY *a little complex* | PREPARATION TIME *about 2 hours*

PASTRY
100 g butter, cold
200 g all-purpose flour
100 g caster sugar
2 egg yolks
1½ tbsp cold water

FILLING
250 g mascarpone
250 g low-fat cream cheese
1 tsp vanilla paste
3 tbsp icing sugar
3 tbsp cream
1 box (80 g) strawberry jelly
   powder
190 ml hot water
1,2 kg small strawberries

Prepare the pastry by rubbing the butter into the flour using your fingertips. Add the caster sugar and mix well. Beat the egg yolks lightly and add to the mixture, along with the water, to form a dough. Knead lightly until smooth and refrigerate for 15 minutes.

Preheat the oven to 190 °C.

Grease a 30-cm tart tin and roll out the pastry on a lightly floured surface. Line the tart tin with the pastry and press down lightly. Chill for a further 25 minutes.

Line the base of the pastry with baking paper and ceramic baking beans (or just old-fashioned dry beans) and bake for 15 minutes before reducing the heat to 150 °C and baking for a further 10 minutes. Remove the baking paper and beans, and bake for 10 more minutes.

Remove from the oven and allow to cool.

In the meanwhile, mix the mascarpone, cream cheese, vanilla paste, icing sugar and cream until smooth.

Prepare the jelly by adding the hot water to the jelly powder and stirring until the sugar has dissolved. Set aside to cool a little.

To assemble the tart, make sure that the pastry casing is completely cold. Spread the creamy filling over the base of the tart. Cut the tops off the strawberries to give them a base on which to stand. When the jelly starts to thicken, toss the strawberries in the jelly mixture and arrange the strawberries on top of the creamy filling. Pour the rest of the jelly onto the base and allow to set before serving.

Strawberry flan

VINAGRE DE PINA (PINEAPPLE VINEGAR)

(v) | (GF) | MAKES *1 litre* | DIFFICULTY *quick and easy*
PREPARATION TIME *30 minutes (plus 4 weeks to ferment)*

55 g sugar
1 litre purified water
peel of 1 very ripe organic
    pineapple

COOK'S NOTE: Vinagre de pina, or
pineapple vinegar, is used in Mexican
cooking as part of a salad dressing, or as a
marinade for meat, poultry and fish.

Place the sugar and water in a glass bowl and stir until the sugar dissolves. Place the pineapple peel in a 1-litre (or more) glass jar and cover with the liquid. Cover the top with cheesecloth to keep the fruit flies at bay, and leave to ferment at room temperature in a warm, draught-free spot.

When the liquid begins darkening after about 1 week, strain out the peel and discard. If the liquid has not changed colour, leave for a little longer.

Ferment the liquid for 2 to 3 weeks longer, agitating periodically.

PINEAPPLE AND ROSEMARY JAM

(v) | (GF) | MAKES *500 g* | DIFFICULTY *easy* | PREPARATION TIME *about 1¾ hours*

1 large pineapple
250 ml water
500 ml sugar
juice of 3 limes
115 g granadilla pulp
¼ tsp rosemary, very finely
    chopped

COOK'S NOTE: The jam can be kept in
the refrigerator for up to 3 months.

Peel the pineapple and grate the flesh – you should end up with 2 cups (500 ml). Place the pineapple and water in a small saucepan and cook over medium to low heat until the pineapple is soft – about 20 minutes.

Add the sugar, lime juice, granadilla pulp and rosemary and stir to combine. Cook until the mixture has thickened – about 1 hour.

Spoon the hot jam into a sterilised jar with a tight-fitting lid. Store in the fridge.

Pineapple and rosemary jam

GALETTE DES ROIS

(v) | SERVES *4 to 6* | DIFFICULTY *a little complex*
PREPARATION TIME *about 1½ hours (plus 1¾ hours' refrigeration)*

PASTRY
500 g puff pastry, ready-made
1 large egg yolk, beaten with
    1 tsp water, to glaze

PINEAPPLE FILLING
1 small pineapple, peeled, cored
    and finely chopped
1 tbsp yellow sugar

CREAM
75 g unsalted butter, softened
75 g icing sugar
75 g ground almonds
2 large organic or free-range
    eggs (1 for the cream and 1
    for glazing)
1 large organic or free-range
    egg yolk
1 tbsp dark rum

COOK'S NOTE: The term galette des rois
literally translates as 'cake for kings'.
This tart is traditionally served in France
at New Year's parties. A coin is placed
inside the tart, and tarts are sold with
sturdy paper crowns on top. Whoever is
lucky enough to stumble upon the coin
gets to be king (or queen) for the day.
I've added the pineapple here as a twist.

On a lightly floured work surface, roll out the puff pastry to a thickness of about 2 mm. Cover with cling film and refrigerate for 30 minutes to firm and prevent shrinkage while cooking.

Remove the pastry from the fridge and cut out 2 x 20 cm circles, using a plate or cake tin as a template, and refrigerate for at least another 30 minutes to help it keep its shape during baking.

Place the pineapple and yellow sugar in a small pan, and cook until the sugar has dissolved and the liquid has reduced. Set aside to cool completely.

Preheat the oven to 180 °C.

Prepare the almond cream by whisking the soft butter and icing sugar to a cream in a large bowl. Gradually mix in the ground almonds, then the egg, egg yolk and rum. Mix until smooth and then refrigerate for 30 minutes.

Line a baking tray with baking paper. Remove the pastry from the fridge and place 1 disc of pastry on the paper. Spoon the almond cream into the centre of the disc and, using a palette knife, spread the cream in a circle, making sure to leave a 4-cm border all round. Top with pineapple. Brush the strip with the beaten egg glaze. Do not brush the glaze onto the outside edge of the pastry as it will prevent it from rising.

Continued on page 86

Galette des rois ('cake for kings')

Continued from page 84

Place the second disc of pastry neatly on top, gently securing it by pressing very gently down onto the pastry. Brush the top of the galette with the beaten egg yolk glaze and refrigerate for 10 minutes. Then repeat the glazing process to give a richer colour. Using a sharp, small paring knife start scoring from the centre of the pastry to create an attractive pattern. Refrigerate for a further 10 minutes.

Bake for 30 to 45 minutes until golden brown. Serve hot.

MARQUISE À L'ANANAS (PINEAPPLE ICE CREAM)

(V) | (GF) | SERVES *4* | DIFFICULTY *moderate* | PREPARATION TIME *50 minutes (plus freezing time)*

2 small, ripe pineapples
sugar for sprinkling
240 ml pineapple juice
120 ml water
230 g sugar
zest and juice of 1 lemon
240 ml cream, whipped

Cut the pineapples in half lengthways, leaving the green tops on. Using a fork, scrape the flesh and juice into a bowl, but discard the core. Be very careful not to break the shell. Then sprinkle the insides of the shells with a little sugar and refrigerate.

Chop up the flesh of the pineapples and add the juice, water, sugar and lemon zest. Bring to the boil and simmer for 5 minutes. Strain and add the lemon juice.

Allow to cool and then place in the freezer for 30 minutes. Remove and break the crystals using a fork. Return to the freezer, and repeat until the mixture resembles small flakes.

Remove from the freezer and whisk using a fork. Fold in the whipped cream and return to the freezer. When frozen, spoon scoops of the ice cream into the chilled pineapple shells.

Serve immediately.

Marquise à l'ananas (pineapple ice cream)

$\mathcal{A}$UTUMN

— • —

— • —

Autumn, in my mother's kitchen, was a time for stocking up. I remember bottling quince preserve to serve with our game pies in winter. During breaks from schoolwork and time with Mom in the kitchen, I would take my little red bicycle and race as fast as I could through all the autumn leaves that had fallen to the ground.

Stuffed and baked whole quince (recipe on page 90)

STUFFED AND BAKED WHOLE QUINCE

(v) | SERVES *4 to 8* | DIFFICULTY *easy* | PREPARATION TIME *1½ hours*

4 quinces, washed, dried and
  cored (using an apple corer)
2 tbsp butter, melted
4 tsp almonds, diced
4 tsp bread crumbs, toasted
2 tsp raisins
¼ tsp vanilla paste
2 tsp creamy blue cheese
2 tsp honey
4 small cinnamon quills

Preheat the oven to 180°C.

Cut the tops and bottoms off the quinces and place them on
a sheet of baking paper on a baking tray.

Mix the rest of the ingredients (except the cinnamon)
together and stuff the cavity made in each of the quinces as
tightly as possible. Push a cinnamon quill into each hole and
place on the baking tray in the oven. Bake for about 1 hour.

Remove and serve warm with custard.

See image on page 89.

LAMB KNUCKLE CURRY WITH QUINCE

(GF) | SERVES *4* | DIFFICULTY *easy* | PREPARATION TIME *2 hours*

3 tbsp olive oil
1 large onion, chopped
2 cloves garlic, crushed
1 tbsp medium-strength curry
  powder
2 sticks cinnamon
1 can (400 g) chopped, peeled
  tomato
1½ tbsp sugar
800 g lamb knuckles
500 ml water
salt and pepper to season
2 small quinces, peeled and
  cored

Heat the olive oil in a pot and fry the onion until it begins to
brown. Add the garlic and fry lightly until just transparent.
Sprinkle the curry powder over the onion mixture and add
the cinnamon sticks. Fry to release the flavours.

Add the can of tomatoes, along with the sugar and fry for
about 5 minutes. Add the lamb knuckles and 1 cup of water
and cook for 30 minutes until cooked dry. Season and then
add the quince and the rest of the water. Allow to simmer
for 1 hour until tender.

Serve on a bed of basmati rice.

Lamb knuckle curry with quince

DECONSTRUCTED QUINCE CRUMBLE

(v) | SERVES *8 to 12* | DIFFICULTY *moderate* | PREPARATION TIME *1 hour (plus time for cooling)*

FILLING
8 quinces, peeled, cored and cut
　into slices
340 g sugar
750 ml water
generous pinch of saffron

CRUMBLE
100 g salted butter
150 g cake flour
75 g caster sugar
1 tbsp water

TOPPING
250 g cream cheese
125 g crème fraîche
1 tbsp icing sugar
¼ tsp vanilla paste

Preheat the oven to 180 °C.

For the filling, place the quinces, sugar, water and saffron in a saucepan and bring to the boil. Lower the heat and allow to simmer for 30 minutes. Remove from the heat and set aside.

To make the crumble, rub the butter into the flour with your fingertips until it resembles bread crumbs. Stir in the caster sugar. Sprinkle the crumbs with the water and stir through lightly with a fork. Scatter on a tray lined with baking paper and bake until golden brown. Remove from the oven and allow to cool. If you are not using immediately, seal in an airtight container.

For the topping, mix the cream cheese and crème fraîche until smooth. Add the icing sugar to sweeten. Mix in the vanilla paste.

To assemble, arrange the crumbs in the bottom of a glass, top with the quince filling and some of its syrup, and then a dollop of the creamy topping.

Deconstructed quince crumble

MEMBRILLO (QUINCE PASTE)

(V) | (GF) | MAKES *750 g* | DIFFICULTY *moderate* | PREPARATION TIME *3 hours*

2 quinces, washed and cut into
   chunks
1 vanilla pod, split
rind of 1 lemon, cut into strips
water for boiling
caster sugar
lemon juice, freshly squeezed
1 tbsp rosewater
melted butter for brushing

COOK'S NOTE: Membrillo can successfully
be stored in the refrigerator, wrapped in
baking paper and then in foil, for up to
12 months.

Place the quince, vanilla pod and lemon rind in a large
saucepan and cover with water to about 2 cm above the
quince. Boil for about 1 hour until quince is tender. Remove
from the heat and use a slotted spoon to remove the quince
from the lemon rind water. Discard the liquid and lemon
rind, but retain the vanilla pod.

Use your fingers to remove – and discard – the pips and
the hard core. Place the quince in a bowl and purée using a
stick blender. Measure the amount of purée and add an equal
amount of caster sugar. Add 1 teaspoon lemon juice for each
cup of purée. Scrape out the seeds from the vanilla pod and
add to the mixture, along with the rosewater.

Return to the saucepan and simmer over medium heat for
1 to 1½ hours, stirring frequently to keep the mixture from
burning. The paste will thicken and turn a deep ruby red.

Line a baking dish with baking paper and brush the paper
with butter. Pour the paste into the dish and smooth out.
Top with another sheet of greased baking paper, cool and
refrigerate overnight.

Serve as a sweet, or as part of a cheese platter.

Membrillo (quince paste)

PEARS WRAPPED IN PASTRY

(v) | SERVES *6* | DIFFICULTY *a little complex* | PREPARATION TIME *2½ hours*

200 g cake flour
125 g butter, cut into chunks
2 tbsp cold water
6 small pears
2 tbsp butter
250 ml port wine
4 tbsp caramel sugar (plus extra
   for sprinkling)
milk for brushing
6 sprigs of thyme for serving

COOK'S TIP: When making the dough,
you may need to add a little more water,
so that it's not sticky. Do not handle
the dough too much because this will
toughen it.

Preheat the oven to 200 °C.

Place the flour in a bowl. Rub the chunks of butter into the flour using your fingertips, until they resemble large bread crumbs. Stir in the cold water. Bring the mixture together to form a ball that is firm but not sticky. Place the pastry in a plastic bag and chill while you prepare the fruit.

Peel the pears, leaving the stems on, and slice off the bottom of each so that they stand on the baking tray. Heat the butter in a saucepan and add the port wine and caramel sugar. Stir until the sugar has dissolved. Add the pears and cook on a medium heat, about 5 minutes per side. Remove from the sauce and set aside to cool and drain.

Once the pears have cooled, take the pastry out of the fridge, divide into 6 equal portions, and roll out into rough circles. Sprinkle each circle with a little caramel sugar, and place a pear in the middle of each. Fold the edges of the pastry up the sides of each pear, as far as it will go (about halfway), and press the pastry so that it fits as snugly around the pear as possible. Brush the outside of each pastry shell with milk.

Place in the preheated oven and bake for about 40 minutes until the pastry is golden brown. To serve, drizzle each pear with some of the heated syrup and decorate with a sprig of thyme. Serve warm.

Pears wrapped in pastry

PEAR AND CHOCOLATE CAKE

(v) | (GF) | SERVES *12* | DIFFICULTY *moderate* | PREPARATION TIME *1¾ hours*

185 g gluten-free self-raising
   flour
3 pinches of salt
30 g cocoa powder
250 g unsalted butter
95 g caster sugar
95 g muscovado sugar
250 g good-quality dark
   chocolate
185 ml black coffee (plunger
   or filter)
185 ml water
2 eggs, beaten lightly
2 large pears, peeled, cored
   and quartered

COOK'S NOTE: This cake is moist and can
be served as dessert. Serve with a dollop
of Greek yoghurt, whipped cream or
crème fraîche.

Preheat the oven to 180 °C.

Spray a ring-form tin with non-stick cooking spray and set aside.

Sift the flour, salt and cocoa together.

Place the butter, caster and muscovado sugar, chocolate, coffee and water in a thick-bottomed saucepan and stir over low heat until melted, thick and glossy. Allow to cool for 15 minutes.

Stir the mixture into the dry ingredients and beat well until smooth. Whisk the eggs lightly in a bowl and then beat into the mixture. The mixture should be runny.

Place the pear quarters in the bottom of the ring-form tin, with their rounded sides facing down. Pour the chocolatey mixture into the tin.

Place into the preheated oven and bake for 40 to 45 minutes. When cooked, the top will be firm and slightly cracked.

Remove from the oven and leave to cool. Remove from the tin and place onto a serving platter.

Pear and chocolate cake

PEAR AND GORGONZOLA GNOCCHI

(v) | SERVES *4 as a starter* | DIFFICULTY *quick and easy* | PREPARATION TIME *30 minutes*

4 litres water
salt
2 pears, halved, cored and cut
  into slices
2 leeks, washed well and finely
  sliced
50 g butter (plus extra for
  coating the gnocchi)
200 ml fresh cream
200 g Gorgonzola
sprinkling of ground nutmeg
500 g gnocchi
black pepper, freshly milled

Bring 4 litres of salted water to the boil.

Fry the pear slices and leeks in the butter until the leeks start browning, then set aside. Place the cream and Gorgonzola in the same saucepan and melt over a medium heat. Add the nutmeg to the mixture while still in the pan.

Place the gnocchi in the boiling water and simmer for about 2 minutes or until they float to the surface. Drain and coat with 1 tablespoon of butter.

Pour the sauce over the gnocchi and toss lightly. Top with the pears, leeks and black pepper. Serve immediately.

Pear and Gorgonzola gnocchi

PEAR AND RICOTTA PHYLLO TARTS

(v) | SERVES *6* | DIFFICULTY *moderate* | PREPARATION TIME *1 hour*

15 g butter, melted (for brushing)
300 g fresh ricotta
5 tsp caster sugar
½ tsp vanilla paste
3 pears, stemmed, peeled and cored
1 tbsp butter
5 tsp treacle sugar
zest of 1 lemon
1 tbsp walnuts, chopped
1 tbsp currants
3 sheets phyllo pastry
icing sugar for dusting

Preheat the oven to 180 °C.

You will need 6 individual loose-bottomed tartlet dishes or a 6 x ½-cup-capacity muffin tray. Brush lightly with melted butter and set aside.

Place the ricotta, caster sugar and vanilla paste in a bowl and mix until combined. Set aside.

Cut the pears into slices, keeping the tip intact so that you can fan them later onto the tartlet bases. Place the butter and sugar in a pan over medium heat and stir until the sugar has dissolved. Add the pears and gently toss, coating them in the butter-and-sugar mixture. Once the pears begin to caramelise, add the lemon zest, walnuts and currants, and cook on a low temperature until the currants are plump – about 2 minutes. Remove from the heat.

Lay the phyllo out on a dry surface. Place a damp dishcloth on top of the phyllo to prevent it from drying out. Cut each sheet into 6 squares and brush each square lightly with butter. Position each square at 30 degree angles, using 3 squares per tartlet. Place these into the muffin tin. Bake for about 5 to 10 minutes or until they just turn golden brown. Remove from the oven and cool on a wire rack.

Fill the tartlet shells with the ricotta mixture and then top with the caramelised pear mixture. Place the filled tartlets back into the oven and bake for 10 to 15 minutes.

Serve on individual plates and dust lightly with icing sugar. Serve immediately.

Pear and ricotta phyllo tarts

SWEET VANILLA RISOTTO WITH POACHED PLUMS AND CHOCOLATE

(V) | (GF) | SERVES 6 | DIFFICULTY *moderate* | PREPARATION TIME *1 hour*

6 ripe plums, halved and stones
   removed
6 tbsp caster sugar
1 stick cinnamon
zest and juice of 1 orange
85 g butter
2 vanilla pods
325 g Arborio rice
125 ml white wine
1 litre full-cream milk
100 g best-quality 70% dark
   chocolate, snapped into pieces

Place the plums in a small saucepan with 4 tablespoons of the sugar, the cinnamon, and the orange zest and juice. Cover with a lid and slowly simmer for 10 to 15 minutes. They should be soft but still hold their shape. Remove from the heat and put to one side.

Melt two thirds of the butter in a thick-bottomed saucepan. Score down the length of the vanilla pods and remove the fragrant seeds by scraping a knife down the inside of each half. Add the seeds to the butter and stir. Continue to cook for 1 minute before adding the rice and the remaining sugar.

Turn the heat up to medium, stir the rice, and add the wine, continuing to stir until the wine has almost cooked away. Now add the milk little by little. Keep the rice on a slow but constant simmer for about 20 minutes and stir continuously to form a silky, creamy and classic Italian risotto.

When the rice has cooked through (each grain should be creamy on the outside and firm in the middle), you may need to add a little more milk to adjust the consistency.

Remove from the heat and add the rest of the butter, gently stirring it into the mixture. Place the lid on top, and leave for 3 minutes.

Discard the cinnamon stick, and spoon the risotto onto plates. Push a couple of pieces of dark chocolate into the middle of each helping. Gently place the plums on the risotto, then drizzle with some of the syrupy juice.

Sweet vanilla risotto with poached plums and chocolate

PLUM COBBLER INFUSED WITH ROOIBOS TEA

(v) | (GF) | SERVES 6 | DIFFICULTY *easy* | PREPARATION TIME *about 50 minutes*

COBBLER

6 plums, stones removed, and
  cut into slices
5 tbsp caster sugar
1 rooibos tea bag steeped in
  100 ml boiling water

FILLING

6 heaped tbsp butter, chilled
225 g gluten-free self-raising
  flour
5 tbsp caster sugar (plus extra
  for dusting)
large pinch of salt
130 ml buttermilk
double-thick cream for serving
  (optional)

Preheat the oven to 190 °C.

Place the plums in a pan with the caster sugar and a good glug of the rooibos tea. Cook gently until the plums' juices begin to run. Place into an oven dish or into individual oven-proof cups.

Prepare the topping by rubbing the cold butter into the flour, using your fingertips, until the mixture resembles fine bread crumbs. Add the rest of the caster sugar and the salt, and mix into the flour mixture before adding the buttermilk to form a loose scone-type mixture.

Spoon the topping over the hot fruit and sprinkle with a little caster sugar. Bake in the preheated oven for 30 minutes until golden brown.

Serve hot with double-thick cream.

Plum cobbler infused with rooibos tea

ROASTED PLUMS WITH BROWN-SUGAR MERINGUE SHARDS AND WHITE CHOCOLATE

(V) | (GF) | SERVES *8 to 10* | DIFFICULTY *a little complex*
PREPARATION TIME *45 minutes (plus 4 hours for baking the meringue)*

FRUIT
16 large plums, halved and
    stones removed
3 tbsp brown sugar
finely grated zest and juice of
    2 oranges
melted white chocolate to serve

MERINGUE
2 egg whites
50 g caster sugar
50 g treacle sugar

Preheat the oven to 100 °C.

To make the meringue, whisk the egg whites to soft peaks. Add the caster sugar slowly, beating continuously until it is glossy and thick. Fold the treacle sugar into the mixture.

Line a baking tray with baking paper and spread the meringue mixture onto the paper to a thickness of about 3 to 4 mm.

Place in the preheated oven and bake for 4 hours. Remove and allow to cool.

Turn the oven temperature up to 200 °C.

Place the plums, cut side up, in a roasting dish and sprinkle the brown sugar, zest and juice over them. Bake for 30 minutes.

To assemble, melt white chocolate. Place the plums on a platter and drizzle with the melted chocolate. Break the sheet of meringue into shards and add to the platter.

Serve immediately.

Roasted plums with brown-sugar meringue shards and white chocolate

PLUM PIE

(v) | SERVES *6 to 8* | DIFFICULTY *a little complex*
PREPARATION TIME *about 1¾ hours (plus 2 hours for pastry to rest)*

PIE CRUST

375 g all-purpose flour
300 g unsalted butter, cut into blocks
2 tbsp caster sugar
1 tsp salt
6 tbsp cold water

FILLING

8 large black plums, cut into eighths
180 g yellow sugar
4 tbsp cornflour (Maizena)
2 tbsp water

TO PREPARE THE CRUST FOR BAKING

1 egg
1 pinch of salt
extra yellow sugar for sprinkling

TO SERVE

cream

To prepare the pie crust, rub the butter into the flour using your fingertips. When it resembles bread crumbs, add the caster sugar and salt, and then the water. Press the dough to form a ball, and divide into two. Wrap tightly in cling film and refrigerate for at least 2 hours.

Preheat the oven to 200 °C.

Prepare the filling by placing the plums and the yellow sugar in a saucepan over a medium heat. Mix the cornflour and water to form a smooth paste, and add to the plums. Stir until the sugar has dissolved and allow to simmer for a further 5 minutes to form a thick sauce. Remove from the heat.

Grease a pie dish and roll out the 2 balls of pastry to a thickness of about 5 mm. Place 1 sheet of pastry in the bottom of the pie dish and allow it to drape over the sides. Place the plum filling on the pastry shell and distribute evenly. Now drape the other sheet of pastry on top to form a crust. Cut away all excess pastry and crimp the edges together securely. Cut a few slits in the crust and chill the pie for 20 minutes.

Before baking, whisk the egg and salt together lightly. Brush the pie crust with the egg wash and sprinkle with the extra yellow sugar before placing in the preheated oven on a preheated oven tray (to ensure that the pastry shell cooks from the bottom too).

Bake for 20 minutes at 200 °C and then lower the heat to 180 °C for 25 minutes until the filling bubbles and the crust is golden brown.

Remove from the oven and serve warm with a dash of cream.

Plum pie

BLOOMING ONIONS

(v) | SERVES *4* | DIFFICULTY *a little complex* | PREPARATION TIME *30 minutes*

1 egg
250 ml milk
130 g all-purpose flour
1½ tsp salt
1½ tsp cayenne pepper
1 tsp paprika
½ tsp ground black pepper
¼ tsp dried oregano
generous pinch of dried thyme
generous pinch of ground cumin
4 small sweet onions
vegetable oil for frying

Cook's Tip: The last 8 'petals' will be difficult to cut, so be careful. To help keep the 'petals' separate, plunge the onion into boiling water for 1 minute and then into cold water.

Beat the egg in a bowl and add the milk. In a separate bowl, combine the flour, salt, cayenne pepper, paprika, ground black pepper, oregano, thyme and cumin and mix together.

To prepare the onions, slice 2½ cm off the top and bottom of the onion and remove the papery skin. Use a thin knife or an apple corer to cut a 2½-cm-diameter core out of the middle of the onion. Now use a large, very sharp knife to slice the onion several times down the centre to create 'petals': first slice through the centre of the onion to about three quarters of the way down – but not right down to the bottom. Turn the onion 90 degrees and slice it again in an X across the first slice. Keep slicing the sections in half, very carefully until the onion has been cut 16 times. Do not cut through the onion.

Spread the 'petals' apart, and then dip the onions into the milk mixture and coat them liberally with the flour mixture. Again, separate the petals and sprinkle the dry coating between them. Once the onions are well coated, repeat the process.

Heat the oil in a deep-fryer or deep pot. Make sure you use enough oil to cover the onions completely when they fry.

Fry the onions right side up in the oil for 10 minutes or until brown. Remove from the oil and let them drain on paper towel.

Serve with a steak or lamb chops.

Blooming onions

CARAMELISED ONION TARTLETS

(v) | SERVES *4* | DIFFICULTY *moderate* | PREPARATION TIME *about 50 minutes*

40 g caster sugar
40 ml water
thyme leaves
2 large onions, peeled and cut in
    half widthways
salt and pepper to season
olive oil
1 roll ready-made puff pastry

COOK'S TIP: The caramel will harden
when it gets cold, making it hard to get
out of the tin. If it does, place the tartlets
back in the oven for a minute to melt the
caramel.

Preheat the oven to 200 °C.

Line 4 tartlet baking tins with baking paper.

Place the sugar and water in a pan over medium heat and stir until the sugar has dissolved. Allow to simmer until a golden-brown caramel is formed. It should not be too dark in colour.

Pour the caramel in even quantities into the tartlet tins. It will harden fairly quickly. Sprinkle the top with thyme leaves and place the onions, largest cut side facing down, on top of the caramel. Season with salt and pepper, and brush with a little olive oil before placing the tins on a baking tray into the preheated oven.

Bake for 15 minutes and remove from the oven. Set aside and allow to cool completely.

Cut out 4 pastry circles the size of the tartlet tins and lay over the onion. Bake for 20 minutes until golden brown.

Remove from the oven and carefully flip the tartlets onto plates. Remove the baking paper and serve immediately as a starter or as an accompaniment to a meat dish.

Caramelised onion tartlets

ONION AND PECORINO FOCACCIA

(v) | MAKES *2* | DIFFICULTY *moderate* | PREPARATION TIME *4 hours (including 3 hours' rising time)*

½ tsp caster sugar
2 tsp dried yeast
800 ml lukewarm water
1 kg all-purpose flour
2 tsp salt
2 tbsp olive oil
cornflour (Maizena) for dusting
1 medium-sized onion, cut into
  eighths
100 g pecorino, finely grated
olive oil for brushing

Place the sugar and yeast in a small bowl and stir in 60 ml of water. Leave in a draught-free spot to activate – if the yeast does not bubble and foam within 5 minutes, throw it away and start again.

Mix the flour and salt in a bowl and add the olive oil, yeast mixture and three quarters of the remaining water (555 ml) to the flour and mix. Add the rest of the water, a little at a time until the dough loosely clumps together. Transfer to a lightly floured surface and knead for 8 minutes until smooth.

Rub the inside of a large bowl with olive oil. Rub the ball of dough with olive oil and cut a shallow cross on top of the ball with a sharp knife. Cover the dough with a dishcloth and leave in a draught-free spot for 1 to 1½ hours until doubled in size.

Punch down the dough to its original size and then divide in two. (At this stage the dough can be refrigerated for up to 4 hours, or frozen – but allow to return to room temperature before using.)

Roll each portion into a 28 x 20-cm rectangle. Lightly oil 2 baking trays and dust them with cornflour. Place the dough onto the baking trays and, using the heels of your hands, work from the centre of the dough outwards, to fill each tray. Slide the trays inside 2 plastic bags, seal and leave in a draught-free spot to rise for another 2 hours.

Preheat the oven to 220 °C.

Scatter the onions over the surface of the dough and press them firmly down. Brush the surface with olive oil and sprinkle with the grated pecorino. Bake for 20 minutes or until golden brown.

Onion and pecorino focaccia

PISSALADIÈRE

SERVES 6 | DIFFICULTY *a little complex* | PREPARATION TIME *2½ hours*

PASTRY
225 g all-purpose flour
pinch of salt
225 g cold unsalted butter,
    coarsely grated
6 tbsp iced water

TOPPING
250 ml olive oil
6 large onions, thinly sliced
1 tbsp fresh thyme leaves,
    chopped
20 anchovy fillets
caper berries

COOK'S NOTE: Pissaladière is an onion-
and-anchovy tart originating in Nice,
France.

It is a good idea to retain the drained
oil from the onions and to use it again
in other dishes as it has a wonderfully
beguiling onion-and-thyme flavour.

To make the pastry, sift the flour and salt together on a cold work surface. Scatter the butter over and mix roughly. Form a well in the centre and add the iced water, mixing with a pastry scraper until a dough forms. Cover with cling wrap and refrigerate for 20 minutes.

Roll the pastry out into a rectangle on a lightly floured surface, to a thickness of about 1½ cm, and fold the short ends over to meet in the centre. Fold again, in half, in the same direction, then cover with cling wrap and refrigerate for another 20 minutes. Repeat this rolling-and-resting process twice more.

In the meantime, prepare the topping by heating the oil in a large saucepan and adding the onions and thyme. Reduce the heat to low and cook, stirring occasionally, for 40 minutes. The onions must be soft but not browned.

Preheat the oven to 180 °C.

Line a baking tray with baking paper. Roll out the pastry to a size of 18 x 30 cm and a thickness of about 7 mm. Place the pastry on the baking tray.

Drain the onions as much as possible, retaining the oil (see cook's note), and spread the mixture over the pastry. Drain the anchovies and place in a lattice pattern on top of the onions. Drizzle with a little of the drained oil and place in the oven. Bake for 30 to 40 minutes until puffed and golden brown.

Remove from the oven and place a caper berry in each diamond shape. Serve hot.

Pissaladière

BEEF TERIYAKI SPINACH WRAPS

SERVES *4* | DIFFICULTY *easy* | PREPARATION TIME *about 40 minutes (plus 1 hour for the meat to marinate)*

FILLING
350 g beef fillet, sliced into thin
    strips
6 tbsp teriyaki sauce
2 tbsp soy sauce
2 tbsp sugar
3 tbsp oil
1 whole red onion, thinly sliced
4 cloves garlic, peeled and thinly
    sliced
2 cm ginger, peeled and finely
    grated

WRAPS
4 large leaves of spinach or
    Swiss chard
boiling water
a few drops of sesame oil

Soak the beef in a mixture of the teriyaki sauce, soy sauce and sugar for about 1 hour.

Heat the oil in a wok or frying pan and sauté the onion until transparent. Add the garlic and sauté until fragrant.

Add the meat (with its sauce) and the ginger, and cook until the sauce begins to go sticky. Remove from the heat and set aside.

To make the wraps, wash the spinach and pat dry. Remove the thickest part of the rib and discard. Dip the spinach into the boiling water, 1 leaf at a time, and remove. Place on paper towel to drain and pat dry.

Place 1 spinach leaf on a board at a time and spoon a quarter of the meat in the middle of each leaf. Fold the bottom part over and the sides inward, and roll into a tight wrap.

Heat the sesame oil in a skillet and place the wraps in the hot oil for about 3 minutes. Cut each wrap in two and drizzle with the sauce from the pan before serving.

Beef teriyaki spinach wraps

SPICY PORK, SPINACH AND NOODLE BROTH

SERVES *6 to 8* | DIFFICULTY *easy* | PREPARATION TIME *about 1¼ hours*

200 g pork mince
2 cloves garlic, peeled and finely
    chopped
½ tsp ginger, peeled and finely
    grated
1 tsp Sichuan peppercorns,
    crushed
1 tsp sweet chilli sauce
¼ tsp cumin
¼ tsp lemongrass, finely grated
salt to season
1 tbsp vegetable oil
4 medium-sized leeks, thinly
    sliced
750 ml chicken stock
300 g spinach, torn
2 tbsp soy sauce
1 tsp fish sauce
400 g wide rice noodles
sesame oil for stir-frying

COOK'S TIP: When removing the noodles
from the hot water, make sure that they
have not clumped together – separate if
necessary.

Mix the pork mince, garlic, ginger, Sichuan peppercorns, sweet chilli sauce, cumin, lemongrass, salt and pepper in a medium-sized bowl.

Heat the oil in a stock pot over medium heat. Cook the leeks in the oil until transparent. Add the pork mixture, stirring with a wooden spoon to break up the mince, for about 10 minutes until browned.

Add the stock and bring to the boil. As soon as it begins to boil, reduce the heat and simmer for a further 10 minutes until the flavours have mingled.

Add the spinach, soy sauce and fish sauce and cook, stirring occasionally, until the spinach is tender.

In the meantime, soak the noodles in very hot (not boiling) water from the kettle and then drain. Heat the sesame oil in a wok and, when hot, stir-fry the noodles for a few minutes and season with salt.

Divide the noodles into individual bowls. Ladle the broth into the bowls and serve.

Spicy pork, spinach and noodle broth

BABY SPINACH SALSA VERDE

(GF) | (LC) | SERVES *4* | DIFFICULTY *quick and easy* | PREPARATION TIME *about 45 minutes*

SAUCE
150 g baby spinach
2 spring onions, finely chopped
180 ml extra-virgin olive oil
2 tbsp chives, finely chopped
1 tbsp red wine vinegar
1 tsp lemon zest, finely grated
salt and freshly milled black
    pepper to season

FISH
olive oil for frying
4 small, whole fish
juice of 1 lemon
salt to season

For the salsa verde, chop the spinach leaves finely, stems and all, and combine with the spring onions, oil, chives, vinegar and lemon zest in a medium-sized bowl. Season with salt and pepper and toss to combine. Set aside.

To prepare the fish, heat the olive oil (ideally, in a fish pan). Wash the fish and pat dry. When the oil is hot, cook the fish until just done – in other words, the flesh flakes easily. Squeeze the lemon juice over and season with salt.

To serve, place the salsa verde on the bottom of a plate and top with a fish for each. Serve hot with a crusty loaf.

COOK'S NOTE: You can use fish such as sardines or silverfish. But make sure that you select fish that are caught in a responsible and sustainable manner.

SAUTÉED SPINACH WITH PRESERVED LEMONS

(V) | (GF) | (LC) | SERVES *4* | DIFFICULTY *quick and easy* | PREPARATION TIME *30 minutes*

3 tbsp butter
1 large leek, thinly sliced
300 g spinach, ribs and stems
    removed and leaves torn
1 tbsp preserved lemons,
    chopped (see page 38)
salt and pepper to season

Heat the butter in a skillet and cook the leek until it begins to brown. Add the spinach in batches, tossing and allowing each batch to cook down before adding the next. If the pan cooks dry, add a splash of water.

Add the preserved lemons and toss until the spinach is wilted and tender. Season before serving hot.

COOK'S TIP: This is an excellent accompaniment to roast chicken.

Sautéed spinach with preserved lemons

CRUNCHY BUTTERNUT FRITTERS

(v) | SERVES 6 | DIFFICULTY *easy* | PREPARATION TIME *1½ hours*

450 g butternut, peeled, seeds
   removed and cut into cubes
6 large sage leaves, finely
   chopped
½ tsp salt
65 g all-purpose flour, sifted
1 tsp baking powder
1 egg, beaten
vegetable oil for frying
50 g pine nuts, toasted
50 g feta cheese, crumbled

Steam the cubes of butternut for 30 to 40 minutes or until soft. Set aside to cool.

When cooled, mash the butternut and mix in the sage, salt, flour, baking powder and egg. The consistency should be that of a smooth batter. Allow to stand for 10 minutes.

Cover the base of a frying pan with oil and bring to a medium heat. Place tablespoonfuls of batter into the hot oil and fry until golden brown on both sides. Drain on paper towel.

Serve immediately.

COOK'S TIP: If the oil is too hot when frying, the batter will brown quickly and stay raw in the centre.
   This dish can be served as an accompaniment to lamb, chicken or a game fish.

Crunchy butternut fritters

BUTTERNUT PHYLLO TART

(v) | SERVES *4 to 6* | DIFFICULTY *a little complex* | PREPARATION TIME *1¾ hours*

450 g butternut, peeled and
   seeds removed
sprinkling of ground nutmeg
¼ tsp ground cinnamon
1 tbsp caster sugar
2 tbsp ricotta
2 sheets phyllo pastry
melted butter for brushing
icing sugar for sprinkling
double-thick cream to serve

Preheat the oven to 180 °C.

Steam the butternut for 40 minutes or until soft. Allow to cool.

Mash the butternut using a fork and mix in the nutmeg, cinnamon, caster sugar and ricotta to form a paste.

Lay the phyllo on the counter and cut in half lengthways. Place the pastry under a damp paper towel to keep from drying out. Place a half-sheet of phyllo on the counter and brush lightly with the melted butter. Place another half-sheet on top and overlap the third half-sheet over the edge of the first two, brushing with the butter and topping with the last sheet.

Form a sausage (about 2 cm in diameter) with the butternut paste and place about 5 cm from the bottom and 3 cm from the side of the phyllo. Fold the sides towards the filling and the bottom part of the phyllo over the filling, and brush with the melted butter. Roll the pastry to form a long sausage shape, making sure to brush all areas with the melted butter.

Carefully roll the pastry into a coil and place on a sheet of baking paper. Bake for 30 minutes or until golden brown.

Sprinkle with icing sugar and serve hot or warm as a dessert with a blob of double-thick cream.

Butternut phyllo tart

BUTTERNUT STUFFED WITH RAGÙ

SERVES *4* | DIFFICULTY *easy* | PREPARATION TIME *about 1 hour*

4 small butternuts, tops cut off
   and seeds removed, leaving
   the hollowed 'bowls'
2 tbsp olive oil (plus extra for
   rubbing)
1 small onion, peeled and
   chopped
1 large clove garlic, peeled and
   crushed
250 g minced lamb
200 g tomato purée
salt and freshly milled black
   pepper to season
1 tsp sugar
25 g couscous
pinch of salt
1 tsp butter (plus extra for the
   top)
15 g Parmesan, finely grated

Preheat the oven to 180 °C.

Rub the outside of the butternut with the oil and place, open side down, in a roasting dish. Bake for 40 minutes until soft. Remove from the oven, tip upright and allow to cool.

In the meantime, prepare the ragù by frying the onion in olive oil until it begins to brown. Turn the heat to medium and add the garlic, stirring to make sure that it doesn't turn brown.

Add the minced lamb and fry, stirring continuously to make sure that the meat separates and cooks through. Add the tomato pureé and season with salt and pepper. Add the sugar and cook over a low heat until the mixture has reduced and the flavours have mingled – about 20 minutes.

Add 35 ml boiling water and a pinch of salt to the couscous. Cover and allow to steam for 5 minutes. Toss with a fork to loosen and add the butter and Parmesan. Mix and set aside.

Spoon the ragù into the hollow of the butternut and top with the couscous. Top with a small blob of butter and bake for a further 20 to 30 minutes.

Serve with a tossed salad.

Butternut stuffed with ragù

BUTTERNUT, GORGONZOLA AND DATE QUICHE

(v) | SERVES *8 to 10* | DIFFICULTY *moderate* | PREPARATION TIME *2½ hours*

BASE
125 g butter
125 g all-purpose flour
125 g mature cheddar

FILLING
800 g butternut, peeled and cut
 into small cubes
olive oil for tossing
Maldon salt
3 fresh dates, pitted
200 g pecorino, grated
4 egg yolks
300 ml fresh cream
salt and freshly milled black
 pepper to season
sprinkling of freshly grated
 nutmeg
100 g Gorgonzola

Preheat the oven to 180 °C.

To make the base, rub the butter into the cake flour until the mixture resembles bread crumbs. Add the cheddar and mix, then refrigerate.

For the filling, place the butternut in an oven dish, toss in a little olive oil and sprinkle with Maldon salt. Place in the preheated oven and bake until soft and starting to brown. Remove from the oven and set aside to cool.

Cut each of the dates into 8 strips.

Press the flour mixture on the bottom and up the sides of a loose-bottomed, fluted tart tin, 20 cm in diameter, making sure the mixture is not spread too thick.

Place the cooled butternut in the bottom of the tart tin. Top with the dates and the grated pecorino. Beat the egg yolks into the cream and season with salt and pepper. Add a generous sprinkling of freshly grated nutmeg. Pour the mixture over the butternut. Top with small blobs of Gorgonzola and bake for 30 to 40 minutes, or until golden brown.

Remove and serve warm or at room temperature.

Butternut, Gorgonzola and date quiche

WINTER

—— • ——

—— • ——

Growing up on a farm made it impossible to ignore
the rhythm of the seasons. Winter was potato time
and the three Joseph kids loved nothing better than to
scrape the blackened potatoes out from between the
morning's fiery embers where field workers warmed
their hands, break them open and breathe in the smell
of fluffy potato flesh.

Hasselback potatoes (recipe on page 136)

HASSELBACK POTATOES

(v) | (GF) | SERVES *6* | DIFFICULTY *easy* | PREPARATION TIME *about 2 hours*

12 medium-sized potatoes,
   peeled
200 g butter, melted
salt to season
fresh sage leaves

COOK'S TIP: To ensure you don't cut
right through the potato, place a chop-
stick on each side of it to stop the knife
reaching the cutting surface.

Preheat the oven to 180 °C.

Use a sharp knife to cut thin, even slices in the potato
without cutting all the way through. Fan the slices open
by pressing gently on the cut surface. When done, rub the
potatoes with the melted butter and season with salt. Add
a couple of fresh sage leaves and place in the oven to cook
until soft and golden – about 1½ to 2 hours.

Serve with roast chicken or roast leg of lamb, or as a
healthier alternative to chips.

See image on page 135.

POTATO GRATIN

(v) | (GF) | SERVES *4 to 6* | DIFFICULTY *easy* | PREPARATION TIME *about 1½ hours*

4 large potatoes, peeled
500 ml low-fat cream
sea salt and freshly milled black
   pepper
grated nutmeg to season
handful of chives, finely
   chopped
Parmesan, grated for topping

COOK'S TIP: Use a mandolin to cut the
potato so that the slices are very thin.

Preheat the oven to 180 °C.

Cut the potatoes into very thin slices. Grease an oven-proof
dish and arrange the potato slices in a layer, overlapping
slightly. Repeat the layering process until you have used all
the slices.

Season the cream with sea salt, freshly milled black pepper
and ground nutmeg before pouring over the potatoes. Top
with the chopped chives and a layer of grated Parmesan.

Bake for 45 to 60 minutes, or until the potatoes are soft and
the top has browned.

Serve with chicken, lamb, beef or fish.

Potato gratin

POTATO CROQUETTES

(v) | MAKES *30* | DIFFICULTY *moderate* | PREPARATION TIME *1¼ hours*

8 medium to large potatoes,
  peeled and cut into cubes (for
  4 cups mashed potatoes)
2 tbsp milk
salt and freshly milled black
  pepper to taste
1 tbsp chives, finely chopped
3 tbsp all-purpose flour
3 eggs (1 whole and 2 separated,
  retaining the yolks only)
handful of bread crumbs,
  toasted
vegetable oil for deep-frying

Steam the potato cubes until they are soft, then drain and mash.

Beat the egg yolks and add that, with the milk, salt, pepper, chives and flour, to the mashed potato. Chill and then shape into sausages of 5 to 7 cm.

Beat the whole egg, then dip each croquette in the beaten egg, and roll in the bread crumbs. Allow to rest for 15 minutes.

Fry each croquette in oil until brown on all sides.

COOK'S TIP: Cook in small batches, giving each croquette enough space so that it does not crumble while frying.

Potato croquettes

CAULIFLOWER AND CHICKPEA BIRYANI

(V) | (GF) | SERVES *4* | DIFFICULTY *quick and easy* | PREPARATION TIME *40 minutes*

YOGHURT

2 tbsp mint, finely chopped

1 tbsp lemon juice

250 ml natural yoghurt

salt to season

BIRYANI

300 g basmati rice

2 sticks cinnamon

4 green cardamom pods

salted water

½ head (about 350 g)
    cauliflower, cut into florets

3 tbsp butter

1 onion, peeled and chopped

2 tsp garam masala

2 tsp turmeric

thumb-sized piece of ginger,
    peeled and thinly sliced

salt to taste

¼ tsp saffron threads

80 g raisins

400 g can chickpeas, rinsed and
    drained

250 ml water

Prepare the minted yoghurt by mixing the finely chopped mint and lemon juice into the yoghurt. Season with salt and refrigerate until needed.

For the biryani, place the rice and half the cinnamon and cardamom pods in a pot and cover with salted water. Allow to simmer for 10 minutes until just tender. Drain and rinse in cold water.

Steam the cauliflower florets for 10 minutes.

Heat the butter in a frying pan over a medium heat. Add the onion and fry until transparent. Add the rest of the cinnamon and cardamom, the garam masala, turmeric and ginger and heat them through, cooking for 4 minutes. Season with salt.

Stir in the saffron, raisins and chickpeas to combine. Add the water and then gently stir in the rice and the cauliflower. Allow to simmer for about 5 minutes until all the flavours and colours have mingled.

Serve with the minted yoghurt.

Cauliflower and chickpea biryani

DEEP-FRIED CAULIFLOWER FLORETS SERVED WITH TAHINI

(V) | (GF) | (LC) | SERVES *6 to 8* | DIFFICULTY *quick and easy* | PREPARATION TIME *30 minutes*

SAUCE
80 ml tahini
60 ml water
60 ml fresh lemon juice
1 tbsp parsley, chopped
2 cloves garlic, peeled and
    crushed
salt and milled black pepper

CAULIFLOWER
vegetable oil for deep-frying
1 head cauliflower (about 800 g),
    cut into medium-sized florets

To make the tahini sauce, mix all the ingredients together.
Place in the refrigerator until ready to use.

Heat the oil in a saucepan over a medium to high heat until
hot. Place the cauliflower florets into the oil and fry until
golden brown. Remove from the oil with a slotted spoon
and drain on paper towel.

Place on a serving platter and drizzle with the tahini. Serve
immediately.

COOK's TIP: To test the temperature of the oil, drop a cube of bread into the
oil – if it sizzles and goes golden brown, then the oil is hot enough.

CAULIFLOWER CROQUE MONSIEUR

(GF) | (LC) | MAKES *2 'sandwiches'* | DIFFICULTY *quick and easy* | PREPARATION TIME *30 minutes*

1 head cauliflower
1 tsp Dijon mustard
4 slices of smoked ham
100 g Gruyère, grated
4 tbsp butter, melted

Preheat the oven to 180 °C on the grill setting.

Cut the head of cauliflower to form 4 'slices' of about 1 cm
thick, starting just off the middle where all the florets are
joined. Spread each slice with mustard and place 2 of the
slices on baking paper on an oven tray. Top each of these
with 2 slices of ham, and half the Gruyère, divided between
the 2 slices. Place the other 2 slices of cauliflower on top of
each of these to close the 'sandwiches', and brush generously
with butter.

Place on a sheet of baking paper on an oven tray under the
grill for 10 to 15 minutes until they have begun to brown.
Turn the sandwiches over and sprinkle the rest of the cheese
on top of the cauliflower sandwiches. Place back under the
grill until golden brown – another 10 to 15 minutes. Serve hot.

Cauliflower croque monsieur

SHEPHERD'S PIE WITH CAULIFLOWER MASH

(GF) | (LC) | SERVES *4* | DIFFICULTY *easy* | PREPARATION TIME *1¾ hours*

FILLING

1 large onion, peeled and
  chopped
3 tbsp olive oil
2 cloves garlic, peeled and
  crushed
750 g minced lamb
125 ml water
2 carrots, peeled and cut into
  rounds
salt and pepper to season

TOPPING

about 750 g cauliflower
4 tbsp butter (plus extra for
  grilling)
generous sprinkling of ground
  nutmeg
salt and white pepper to season
80 g Parmesan, finely grated

To make the pie filling, fry the onion in the olive oil until it begins to brown. Add the garlic and fry lightly until transparent. Add the mince and water and stir continuously until loose and cooked. Add the carrots, and season with salt and pepper. Cover and cook on a medium-low heat for 45 minutes.

Preheat the oven to 180° C.

To make the topping, wash the head of cauliflower and shake off excess water. Cut the cauliflower into separate florets and steam for 15 minutes until soft. Place the florets in a bowl and add the butter, nutmeg, salt and pepper and blend with a stick blender until smooth.

Dish the pie filling into individual oven-proof bowls and top with the cauliflower mash. Add a small blob of butter to the top, and sprinkle the grated Parmesan over that. Place in the preheated oven for 30 minutes. The juices will begin to bubble. Turn the oven to the grill setting for a further 5 minutes to brown the cheese.

Serve with green vegetables.

Shepherd's pie with cauliflower mash

CRACKED BLACK PEPPER BEETROOT CRISPS

(v) | (GF) | SERVES *4* | DIFFICULTY *a little complex* | PREPARATION TIME *about 2 hours*

4 large beets, peeled and cut
    into 2-mm-thick slices
2 tbsp olive oil
cracked black pepper

COOK'S TIP: The crunchiness of the
crisps will vary, depending on how thickly
you slice the beetroot and how much oil
you use. I recommend using a mandolin
to keep the slices thin and consistent.

    When the raw beetroot slices are
baked, they shrink considerably, so use
large beets.

    To avoid staining your hands, wear
plastic gloves.

Preheat the oven to 110°C.

Line a few baking trays with baking paper. Then toss the beetroot slices in the oil, making sure they are coated evenly, and pack the slices in a single layer on the baking trays – as many slices as you can fit onto a tray at a time. Sprinkle with the cracked black pepper.

Place in the oven and bake until crisp for about 2 hours, rotating halfway through the process. They should not go brown. When they are crisp, remove from the oven and cool. Blot off all excess oil with paper towel.

BEETROOT HUMMUS

(v) | (GF) | SERVES *12 (about 2 cups)* | DIFFICULTY *quick and easy* | PREPARATION TIME *45 minutes*

300 g beetroot
olive oil to roast and serve
Maldon salt
400 g canned chickpeas (240 g
    drained)
4 large cloves garlic, crushed
6 tbsp tahini
60 ml fresh lemon juice
¼ tsp ground cumin
60 ml olive oil

Preheat the oven to 180°C.

Peel the beetroot and cut into quarters. Toss in olive oil and sprinkle with Maldon salt. Place in the oven and roast for about 30 minutes or until tender. Remove from the oven and set aside to cool.

Drain the chickpeas, retaining some of the liquid, and place them in a blender. Add the garlic to the chickpeas, along with the tahini, lemon juice, cumin and oil. Add the beets and blend until the mixture has combined, adding some of the liquid from the canned chickpeas a drizzle at a time, to get a smooth consistency. Drizzle with olive oil and serve as part of a *mezze* platter.

Beetroot hummus

BEETROOT ORZOTTO WITH HORSERADISH CREAM AND WATERCRESS

(v) | SERVES *4 to 6* | DIFFICULTY *moderate* | PREPARATION TIME *1½ hours*

3 baby beets, peeled
4 large cloves garlic, unpeeled
olive oil for roasting
1 litre vegetable stock
4 tbsp butter (plus 1 tbsp extra)
1 medium-sized onion, peeled
   and finely chopped
300 g pearl barley
150 ml dry white wine
100 g Parmesan, finely grated

TO SERVE
4 tbsp creamed horseradish
125 ml sour cream
watercress

Preheat the oven to 180 °C.

Toss the beets and the cloves of garlic in the olive oil and roast for 30 minutes or until tender. Remove from the oven and set aside, retaining the roasted garlic cloves.

Use a stick blender to blend the stock and the roasted beets. When blended well, heat the mixture in a pot.

While the stock is heating, melt the butter in a saucepan, add the onion and cook until it begins to brown. Squeeze the garlic paste from the roasted cloves into the saucepan and cook for a minute before adding the pearl barley. Cook for about 3 to 5 minutes, stirring. Add the wine and simmer, stirring continuously until almost all of it has been absorbed.

Lower the heat to medium. Add a ladleful of stock at a time, stirring until it has been absorbed, and then add another ladleful. Continue the process for 40 minutes until the pearl barley is cooked, but al dente. You might not need all the stock, but make sure the pot is not too dry – your orzotto needs to be a little more liquid. Stir in the extra tablespoon of butter and the Parmesan. Allow to rest for a few minutes. If your dish is too dry, it will tend to go stodgy at this point.

Mix the horseradish and sour cream in a separate bowl. Remove the stalks from the watercress. Serve the orzotto in bowls, topped with a generous spoonful of the horseradish cream and a handful of the fresh watercress.

Beetroot orzotto with horseradish cream and watercress

BEETROOT BLINIS SERVED WITH MASCARPONE AND CAVIAR

(v) | MAKES *40* | DIFFICULTY *moderate*
PREPARATION TIME *2 hours (including 1 hour resting time for the batter)*

3 baby beets
olive oil for roasting
160 g all-purpose flour
2 tsp dry yeast
pinch of salt
310 ml milk
2 tbsp butter, melted
3 large eggs, separated and
    keeping only 2 egg whites
vegetable oil for frying
mascarpone to serve
black seaweed caviar to serve
fresh dill to serve

Preheat the oven to 180 °C.

Roast the beets for 30 minutes or until tender. Remove from the oven.

Sift the flour in a large bowl. Add the yeast and the salt. Warm the milk, and, using a stick blender, blend the roasted beetroot into the milk. Make a well in the centre of the flour, pour the warm milk into the well and mix. Beat the batter for a few minutes to get rid of all lumps. Cover the bowl and allow the mixture to stand at room temperature for 1 hour – by then it should have doubled in volume.

After an hour, use a fork to beat the batter and get rid of the yeasty bubbles. Add the melted butter and the egg yolks and mix into the batter.

In a separate bowl, beat the 2 egg whites to form stiff peaks. Fold gently into the batter and set aside for 10 minutes.

Lightly grease a heavy-bottomed frying pan and heat over a medium heat. Test the heat by dropping a teaspoonful of the batter into the pan. If hot enough, the batter will immediately start to bubble. When the pan is hot, spoon tablespoonfuls of the batter into the pan and fry until they bubble on the surface – the undersides should now be brown. Flip them over and cook the other sides until brown, for about 1 minute. Repeat until you have used all the batter.

Serve the blinis with the mascarpone, a dollop of the caviar and a sprig of fresh dill.

Beetroot blinis served with mascarpone and caviar

ROAST SWEET POTATO TARTE TATIN

(v) | SERVES *10 to 12* | DIFFICULTY *moderate* | PREPARATION TIME *1¾ hours*

4 red onions, peeled and
  quartered
125 g butter
50 g treacle sugar
1 large sweet potato, cut into
  chunks
4 medium-sized carrots, peeled
  and cut into chunks
500 g vine tomatoes
1 tsp ground cumin
salt and freshly ground black
  pepper
200 ml verjuice
bunch of fresh rosemary
500 g ready-made puff pastry

Preheat the oven to 200 °C.

Fry the onions in the butter and treacle sugar in an oven-proof frying pan or skillet. Steam the sweet potatoes and carrots for 10 minutes. Add to the onions, along with the tomatoes. Distribute the vegetables evenly. Add the cumin, salt and pepper, verjuice and rosemary. Cook uncovered for 45 to 60 minutes.

Remove the vegetables from the oven – the liquid should have reduced and be sticky and syrupy. Place the pastry over the vegetables and cut to fit the top of the pan, leaving about 1 cm extra around the sides. Return to the oven for 35 minutes until the pastry turns golden brown.

Turn the frying pan upside down onto a serving dish. Serve immediately as an accompaniment to a meat, fish or poultry dish.

Roast sweet potato tarte tatin

SWEET POTATO BAKE

(v) | SERVES *6 to 8 as a side dish* | DIFFICULTY *moderate* | PREPARATION TIME *1¼ hours*

FILLING
500 to 800 g sweet potatoes
olive oil for roasting
salt to season
juice and rind of 2 tangerines

CRUST
50 g butter
25 ml honey
50 g oats
50 g ginger biscuits, crushed

Preheat the oven to 180 °C.

Peel the sweet potatoes and cut them into chunks. Toss them in a little olive oil and sprinkle with sea salt. Roast in the preheated oven until tender. Allow to cool slightly.

In the meantime, finely grate the rind of the tangerines into the bottom of a pie dish. Squeeze the juice into the bottom of the dish.

Make the crust by melting the honey and butter together. Mix the oats and crushed ginger biscuits together, then add the honey-and-butter mixture.

Arrange the sweet potatoes in the bottom of the pie dish and spoon the crust over evenly. Bake for about 15 minutes until golden brown on top.

Serve immediately as an accompaniment to a curry or any meat dish.

Sweet potato bake

SWEET POTATO BREAD

v | MAKES *1 large loaf* | DIFFICULTY *a little complex*
PREPARATION TIME *1¾ hours (plus about 1¾ hours to rise)*

350 g orange sweet potatoes,
   peeled and cut into chunks
20 g active dry yeast
250 ml lukewarm water
115 g sugar
125 g butter, melted
1 egg
1 tsp salt
650 g all-purpose flour
melted butter for greasing

Steam the sweet potatoes for 20 minutes, drain, mash and set aside.

Dissolve the yeast in the lukewarm water in a large bowl. Let it stand for 5 minutes to activate. Beat in the mashed sweet potatoes, sugar, butter, egg, salt and half of the flour. Then begin adding the remaining flour, a little at a time, to form a stiff dough.

Turn the dough out onto a floured surface and knead until smooth and elastic – about 8 minutes. Grease a bowl as well as the dough. Place the dough in the bowl, cover and allow to rise in a warm place until doubled in size – about 1 hour.

Preheat the oven to 180 °C.

Grease a large bread tin with the melted butter and form balls with the dough, about the size of golf balls and slightly elongated. Place them snugly beside one another in the bread tin, cover and leave in a warm place to rise for another 40 minutes.

Bake in the preheated oven for 1 hour until golden brown.

Sweet potato bread

SWEET POTATOES STUFFED WITH CHICKEN CURRY

(GF) | SERVES *4* | DIFFICULTY *easy* | PREPARATION TIME *1½ hours*

4 medium-sized sweet potatoes, washed and patted dry

3 tbsp olive oil

1 medium-sized onion, peeled and chopped

2 cloves garlic, peeled and crushed

1 tbsp medium-strength curry powder

400 g chicken breast fillets, cut into thin strips

125 ml cream

salt and freshly milled black pepper to season

melted butter for brushing

handful of parsley, finely chopped

Preheat the oven to 180 °C.

Place the sweet potatoes on an oven tray and bake for 1 hour until soft.

While the sweet potatoes are in the oven, heat the olive oil in a saucepan and fry the onion until transparent. Add the garlic and heat through. Add the curry powder and fry to release the flavours.

Add the chicken strips and fry for a few minutes before adding the cream. Simmer until tender. Season with salt and pepper.

Remove the sweet potatoes from the oven, brush lightly with melted butter and set aside to cool a little.

To serve, make a cut in the top of the sweet potato and push the long ends in towards the middle, squeezing a little to create a bigger cavity for the filling. Spoon the filling into the cavity and add some of the creamy curry sauce. Garnish with the chopped parsley and serve.

Sweet potatoes stuffed with chicken curry

EXOTIC MUSHROOM TERRINE

SERVES *8 to 10 as a starter* | DIFFICULTY *a little complex*
PREPARATION TIME *about 1¾ hours (including cooling time)*

6 to 8 thin slices of prosciutto
(depending on the size of
your bread tin)
150 g fresh eryngii mushrooms,
left whole
150 g fresh shimeji mushrooms,
sliced
300 g fresh shiitake mushrooms,
sliced
200 g portabellini mushrooms,
sliced
3 tbsp good-quality olive oil
3 tbsp salted butter
30 g chives, finely chopped
5 tbsp pistachios
5 tbsp dried cranberries
4 tbsp tawny port
100 g bread crumbs, toasted
4 eggs, lightly beaten
4 tbsp crème fraîche
Maldon salt and freshly milled
black pepper to season

Preheat the oven to 180 °C.

Line a non-stick bread tin with the slices of prosciutto.
Fry all the mushrooms in the olive oil and butter
until brown and set aside while you fry the chives and
pistachios in the greased pan for about 2 minutes. Place
the mushrooms back into the saucepan, along with the
cranberries. Add the tawny port and cook for 2 minutes.

Remove the mixture from the heat and add the bread
crumbs. Allow the mixture to cool before adding the eggs
and crème fraîche. Season and allow to rest for 15 minutes.

Spoon the mushroom mixture on top of the prosciutto and
level with a spatula. Fold the edges of the prosciutto over
the mixture to make it tidy.

Place in the preheated oven and bake for 20 minutes.
Remove and allow to cool.

Serve at room temperature.

COOK'S TIP: This dish can also be prepared the day before and refrigerated
until needed. Allow to reach room temperature before serving.
Serve with burnt Seville orange marmalade or onion marmalade.

Exotic mushroom terrine

BREAKFAST IN A MUSHROOM

(V) | (GF) | (LC) | SERVES 6 | DIFFICULTY *quick and easy* | PREPARATION TIME *45 minutes*

vine tomatoes (1 vine per
   person)
olive oil to drizzle
Maldon salt and pepper to
   season
6 large black or brown
   mushrooms (find some with
   deep edges)
3 tsp butter
6 eggs, at room temperature
6 tbsp cream
12 tbsp Parmesan, finely grated
handful of parsley, roughly
   chopped

Preheat the oven to 200 °C.

Place the vine tomatoes in a dish, drizzle with olive oil and Maldon salt and roast until the skins burst open. Remove from the oven and set aside.

Remove the stems of the mushrooms by twisting and pulling. Drizzle the bottom of a muffin tray with olive oil and place the mushroom inside. Place half a teaspoon of butter on top of each mushroom and drizzle with more olive oil before placing in the oven to bake for 15 to 20 minutes. Set the oven onto grill.

Remove from the oven and break 1 egg inside each mushroom. Top each with 1 tablespoon cream and 2 tablespoons Parmesan. Season with salt and pepper. Place under the grill for 5 minutes. The egg white might run over the edges.

Remove from the oven, top with roughly chopped parsley and serve with roasted vine tomatoes and a hot, crusty loaf.

Breakfast in a mushroom

VEGGIE BURGER

(v) | SERVES *6* | DIFFICULTY *quick and easy* | PREPARATION TIME *40 minutes*

12 large brown mushrooms
olive oil for roasting
4 courgettes, cut into ribbons
 using a potato peeler
Vietnamese coriander, finely
 chopped
soy sauce

FRITTERS
1 can (410 g) sweetcorn kernels,
 drained
95 g all-purpose flour
1 tsp baking powder
1 tbsp milk
½ tsp salt
cracked black pepper to taste
2 eggs
canola oil for frying

Preheat the oven to 180 °C.

Remove the stems of the mushrooms and rub with olive oil. Place on an oven tray and roast for about 20 minutes.

In the meanwhile, make the fritters by mixing all the fritter ingredients. Heat the oil in a pan and drop spoonfuls into the oil to form fritters the size of the mushrooms. Cook on both sides at a medium heat until golden brown and cooked through. Drain on paper towel.

Drizzle a little oil into the pan and heat. Drop the courgette ribbons into the pan and flash-fry until limp.

Assemble the burger by placing a mushroom on a plate, and then top with a fritter, Vietnamese coriander, and finally the courgette ribbons. Drizzle with soy sauce and serve.

Veggie burger

MUSHROOM BITES

(v) | MAKES *24* | DIFFICULTY *quick and easy* | PREPARATION TIME *45 minutes*

24 button mushrooms
2 tbsp butter (plus extra for
   brushing the pastry)
3 tbsp crème fraîche
3 tbsp Fairview Chevin with
   spring onions
4 tsp smooth apricot jam
4 tsp capers, finely chopped
80 g pecorino, finely grated
1 tsp za'atar
3 sheets of phyllo pastry

COOK'S NOTE: Za'atar is a Middle Eastern spice and herb mix containing sesame seeds, thyme, salt and sumac.

   Serve these with drinks before dinner.

Preheat the oven to 180 °C.

Remove the stems from the mushrooms. Fry both sides in butter until golden and set aside on a paper towel to drain.

Mix the crème fraîche, Chevin, apricot jam, capers, pecorino and za'atar together.

Cut the phyllo pastry into squares of about 10 x 10 cm. Brush the squares with melted butter and place 2 on top of one another. Place a mushroom on top of each square and add a teaspoonful of the filling onto each.

Gather the edges of the pastry to form a parcel. Brush the outside with melted butter and place on a sheet of baking paper.

Bake in the preheated oven until golden brown. Allow to cool slightly and serve while crisp.

Mushroom bites

STICKY ORANGE BABAS WITH VANILLA SYRUP

(v) | SERVES *4 to 8* | DIFFICULTY *a little complex* | PREPARATION TIME *about 2 hours*

BABAS

120 g cake flour (plus extra for
  coating the bowl)
zest of 1 large orange (about
  2 tsp), finely grated
2 tsp caster sugar
10 g dry yeast
60 ml milk, lukewarm
90 g butter, softened
1 egg

SYRUP

200 g sugar
180 ml water
130 ml orange juice
zest of 1 orange, finely grated
1 tsp vanilla paste

TOPPING

peel of 1 orange (use a zester to
  make strands)
boiling water, to cover the zest
50 ml caster sugar
50 ml water

COOK'S NOTE: Used tuna cans, well
cleaned, are perfect for these babas.

To make the babas, grease 4 to 8 (depending on your choice
of size) individual moulds and set aside.

Place the flour, zest, sugar and yeast in the bowl of an
electric mixer fitted with a dough hook. With the motor
running, add the milk, butter and egg, a little at a time. Beat
well for about 5 minutes.

Coat a bowl with the extra sifted flour. Grease your hands
with melted butter and transfer the dough to the bowl, cover
with a damp dishcloth and set aside in a warm place until
doubled in size – about 45 minutes.

Preheat the oven to 180 °C.

Punch down the dough, then divide into the moulds. Cover
and set aside until the dough almost fills the moulds – about
15 minutes.

Bake for 20 minutes until risen, golden and springy to the
touch.

In the meantime, make the syrup by placing all the
ingredients in a saucepan over a medium heat and stirring
until the sugar dissolves. Bring to the boil and boil for about
5 minutes.

As soon as the babas come out of the oven, spoon hot syrup
over them, but keep some of the syrup aside for serving.
Leave to cool slightly, then tip the babas out.

Continued on page 170

Sticky orange babas with vanilla syrup

Continued from page 168

To make the orange-peel topping, pour boiling water over the strands and leave for 3 minutes, then strain. In a saucepan over a low heat, combine the sugar and water, and stir until the sugar dissolves. Add the orange zest and boil until soft – about 5 minutes.

To serve, top the babas with the strands, add the remaining syrup and serve warm.

CREAMY ORANGE TRUFFLES

(v) | (GF) | SERVES *20 to 30* | DIFFICULTY *moderate*
PREPARATION TIME *40 minutes (plus 2 hours' refrigeration)*

60 g butter, melted
zest of ½ an orange, finely
　grated
3 tbsp cream
250 g white chocolate, broken
　into small pieces
½ tsp orange extract
¼ tsp orange-blossom water
40 g icing sugar

Melt the butter in a small saucepan, along with the orange zest, and add the cream. As soon as the mixture begins to boil, remove from the heat and pour into a mixing bowl with the chocolate pieces. Cover and allow to rest for 3 minutes.

Add the orange extract and the orange-blossom water and stir until smooth.

Cover and refrigerate for 2 hours until firm enough to handle.

Place the icing sugar in a bowl and coat your hands with it. Using a teaspoon-sized measuring spoon, scoop balls of the chocolate mixture into your hands and roll into balls, coating liberally with the icing sugar.

Store the truffles in a refrigerator before serving.

Creamy orange truffles

BRANDIED HOT FRUIT SALAD

(V) | (GF) | SERVES *4* | DIFFICULTY *easy* | PREPARATION TIME *1½ hours*

1 orange, washed and cut into
  chunks, leaving the peel on
1 small pineapple, peeled and
  cut into chunks
4 large plums, quartered
1 can (410 g) pear halves in syrup
120 ml of the pear syrup
6 tbsp treacle sugar
3 tbsp butter
4 tbsp good-quality brandy
double-thick cream to serve

Preheat the oven to 180 °C.

Place the orange, pineapple, plums and pears in an oven dish
and drizzle with pear syrup. Sprinkle the treacle sugar over
and top with dollops of butter. Pour the brandy over the
fruit and bake for 1 to 1½ hours until browned and slightly
sticky.

Serve warm with spoonfuls of double-thick cream.

CRUNCHY GRANOLA BREAKFAST TART

(V) | SERVES *4* | DIFFICULTY *a little complex* | PREPARATION TIME *1 hour*

95 g rolled oats
4 tbsp mixed seeds (sunflower,
  pumpkin, linseed and sesame)
pinch of salt
50 g butter, melted (plus 15 g
  extra)
2 tbsp honey
60 ml low-fat cream cheese
180 ml Greek yoghurt
1 tsp vanilla paste
juice of 1 orange
3 tbsp yellow sugar
2 oranges, peeled and cut into
  slices

Preheat the oven to 180° C.

Mix the oats, seeds and salt. Add the melted butter
and honey, and mix. Spray 4 x 12-cm loose-bottomed
pastry cases with non-stick cooking spray and press the
oat mixture into the bottom and up the sides. Bake for
15 minutes until crisp and brown. Remove from the oven
and set aside to cool.

In a separate bowl, mix the cream cheese, yoghurt and
vanilla paste until smooth.

Heat the orange juice, 15 g butter and yellow sugar in a pan
and stir until the sugar dissolves. Add the orange slices and
cook until slightly caramelised.

Spoon the yoghurt mixture into the muesli cases. Place the
caramelised orange slices on top of the yoghurt mixture and
drizzle with the syrup from the pan. Serve immediately.

Crunchy granola breakfast tart

INDEX

ISBN: 978-1-920434-80-9

First edition, first impression 2014

Published by Bookstorm (Pty) Ltd
PO Box 4532
Northcliff 2115
Johannesburg
South Africa
www.bookstorm.co.za

Distributed by On the Dot
www.onthedot.co.za

Edited by Sean Fraser
Proofread by Kelly Norwood-Young
Cover design by mr design
Back cover image by Stephanie Traut
Book design and typesetting by mr design
Printed by Interpak Books, Pietermaritzburg

ACKNOWLEDGEMENTS

For weeks our home was a production facility, a photographic studio, a test
kitchen, a laboratory and a place of decadence, all in one. Paddy and I ate our
supper amongst props, reflectors and ladders, and we learnt that nothing
creates ambience like a candle and a long-stemmed glass of wine. Thank you,
my darling husband, for your patience, your love, your excitement, your insight
and your encouragement!

Friends and family were responsible for a swell of excitement as this pro-
ject progressed and I remain grateful. Thank you, Annerie, Liz and Maddy for
the props you so generously handed over and that lived with us for weeks.

And then I would like to thank my father, Richard Joseph, for teaching me
never to give up. So many times I felt that this was a task too mammoth for
me to handle, and then I would think of him and the many times he kept going
in his life … I admire you! And thank you for the privilege of growing up on a
farm, close to the earth and all it offered.

My dearest friend and mentor, Michael Olivier, had enough faith in my abili-
ties to introduce me to my publisher. Thank you, dear Michael, for everything
you mean to me. And you, Pete Goffe-Wood, for your friendship and kind
words in the foreword to this book.

My wonderful friend Laetitia moved in and dedicated three weeks of her
life to helping me kick-start this process – Laetitia, your labours, your encouragement, and most of all, the de-stressing laughter, were all invaluable!

And then there is Nico, who bought me my magnificent camera – without you,
none of this would have been possible. Thank you for seeing what I failed to see
at the time, and for the camera that has now become an extension of me.

Zuki, with a smile, did the endless stream of dishes and attempted to clean
the house around all the mayhem. Thank you.

Thank you, also, to Louise Grantham, Russell Clarke, and all at Bookstorm,
as well as designer, Marius Roux, and editor, Sean Fraser, for capturing my
dream on these pages.